To Build
the Life You Want,
Create the Work
You Love

# To Build
# the Life You Want,

---

*THE SPIRITUAL DIMENSION
OF ENTREPRENEURING*

---

# Create the Work
# You Love

Marsha Sinetar

*ST. MARTIN'S PRESS*   ◦   *NEW YORK*

TO BUILD THE LIFE YOU WANT, CREATE THE WORK YOU LOVE. Copyright © 1995 by Marsha Sinetar. All rights reserved. Printed in the United States of America. No part of this book may be used or reproduced in any manner whatsoever without written permission except in the case of brief quotations embodied in critical articles or reviews. For information, address St. Martin's Press, 175 Fifth Avenue, New York, N.Y. 10010.

Design by Ann Gold

Library of Congress Cataloging-in-Publication Data

Sinetar, Marsha.
    To build the life you want, create the work you love : the spiritual dimension of entrepreneuring / Marsha Sinetar.
            p.  cm.
        ISBN 0-312-11905-4
        1. New business enterprises. 2. Entrepreneurship—Psychological aspects. 3. Vocational interests. 4. Success in business.
    I. Title.
    HD62.5.S573      1995
    658.4′21—dc20                                                94-40050
                                                                CIP

First Edition: February 1995

10   9   8   7   6   5   4   3   2   1

*For A:* May some bit of truth
in these pages yield up the information
and encouragement you need to create
the life and the work you'll love.

*Every calling is great when greatly pursued.*
—Oliver Wendell Holmes


*Every man has his own vocation. The talent is the call.*
—Emerson

# CONTENTS

# ACKNOWLEDGMENTS

In the course of my research many creative people—entrepreneurs all—contributed their insights. Collectively, their stories improved the practical usefulness of my philosophy that we *find* work we love primarily by intuitive, entrepreneurial means. Everyone's remarks were treated anonymously and often in composite form to insure the widest possible applicability about how inventive people find their place in the scheme of things. Among those interviewed, the following were particularly helpful:

Anita Brown
Karl Bucholz
Bonnie Erickson
Greg Horn
Howard Solomon
Erin J. White

Cathie Leavitt
Linda McQueeny Kalkwarf
Pauline Sullivan Marr
Michael Marr
David Torres

I especially want to thank Elaine Markson for patience and good humor over the interminably long time I took to finish this book. I'm grateful to my lawyer, Dan Raas, for cheerfully enduring numerous contractual stops and starts. I'm indebted to Linda Kalkwarf for meticulously word processing hundreds (or more) of manuscript changes and to Pauline Sullivan Marr for intercepting phone calls while I wrote. Dianne Molvig—*long*-time editor—provided much needed enthusiasm and revision assistance midway along this project, and Jennifer Enderlin, Senior Editor at St. Martin's Press, was most helpful in suggesting ways to make this book more readable.

To Build
the Life You Want,
Create the Work
You Love

# Introduction

*Follow the high-spirited few who meet the
unknown effectively.*

When my book *Do What You Love, The Money Will Follow*
came out, it was a big hit. I was thrilled with its success
but somewhat overwhelmed by the onslaught of reader
mail that followed. Intelligent, presumably affluent, and well-
educated readers expressed their unhappiness about their current
work. They hadn't a clue "how" to make the transition into their
preferred careers. Collectively they pleaded for specific road maps
to their destinations. Their refrain sounded like this:

> For years I've been struggling with the problem of how to
> make the leap from where I am to where I want to be. How do
> I manage this? How did you do it? What courses can I take
> that will tell me what to do? What do you suggest?

Another group didn't know *what* they wanted. A few couldn't
recall ever feeling enthusiastic about anything. Cynical and bitter,
they discounted their potential and called the American dream a
farcical illusion. Lawyers, physicians, psychologists, accountants,
corporate executives, homemakers, teachers, and even members of
the clergy were desperate for guidance. Despite affluence, their lives
seemed devoid of zest and meaning. Many required "parental"

hand-holding in order to move through the currents of personal and occupational change. Artists—starving and highly accomplished ones—beseeched me for marketing tips. They sought a blueprint and a time line for achieving fame, glamour, greater visibility, and, of course, more money.

Yet every so often a brief, cheery note arrived from someone who, independently, transcended his or her personal limits or circumstances to carve out a fulfilling, remunerative niche in life's marketplace. These letters celebrated life and the grand adventure of shaping fruitful, meaningful endeavors. These writers were thrilled to be solving their vocational puzzles on their own—by using their own mind as it was meant to be used. Essentially, they cheered:

> Hurray! I'm actively exploring the farthest frontiers of my own life and I love it. I've never worked harder and I know there are no guarantees; maybe that's part of my enjoyment. Your ideas about work and my actual experience are completely in sync. Write some more.

Gradually I realized that, despite obstacles, such plucky souls possessed a mode of thinking and working that let them *live* the traditional "American dream" (even though some of the letters came from Asia, Canada, Australia, and Europe). They had built their lives on the solid ground of genuine interests, meanings, and values. They demonstrated old-fashioned virtues: thrift; hard work; pride of workmanship; love of service and community. They committed themselves to and invested in their talents. They seemed to work for something larger than self. These values—not merely monetary aims—fueled their drive, raised self-esteem, and ultimately insured occupational achievement. Such individuals were in a minority, but their skills and attitudes, their entrepreneurial mind-set gave them an edge—and a life—that most of those asking me for advice clearly craved. The main premise of this book is that authentic *occupational success* is tied to healthy human development and that its seminal demand is spiritual growth—our cultivation of those inner gifts and forces that renew and animate our creative energies.

In *Do What You Love, The Money Will Follow,* I described a general overview and a psychology for entering a new territory of experience—namely, "right livelihood" or "vocation." These terms represent *holistic* definitions of work, from both East and West, respectively. The Buddha, for example, taught that *right livelihood* was work done consciously, with pure intent and as service. Right livelihood helps us grow as persons while we meet our own needs and those of others. The word *vocation* has similar ancient, spiritual, roots: It means a call or summons and, to writers such as psychiatrist Carl Jung (and myself), our unique way of becoming *particular* persons within the context of society. Periodically, in these pages, I'll repeat this definition of vocation since it serves as linchpin for my holistic, largely spiritual philosophy of entrepreneuring. To be sure, you'll see that all entrepreneurs are not whole, not necessarily "spiritual." Yet, every entrepreneur depends on similar inner faculties.

The entrepreneur's process of working is fast becoming our era's new norm. Given the reality of corporate, government, financial, and technological upheaval in the twenty-first century, our new job security requires healthy entrepreneurial prowess. Be assured that you'll gain lasting "job security" only as you become self-reliant, creatively resourceful and fully engaged with your process of enterprise—whatever you elect to do—and all the more so if you'll tune into your life's *genuine* purposes. Self-reliance, full engagement (what psychiatrist Rollo May calls "creative encounter") with work, our ability to create answers and meaningful goals are spiritual qualities: these come from within you. Who would dare call themselves "successful" without the vitality born of these inner characteristics?

We also gain job security by getting our mind to move beyond the notion that someone *else* should give us a job, find it for us, tell us what to do with our life. Then we'll find our authentic *vocation* and transcend the idea that we have no unique gifts or service to offer others. In this book, I'll explore:

- the inner qualities of ordinary persons who take control of their working lives (rather than letting the effects of corporate changes or shifting circumstances dictate);
- the "success profile" of ordinary people who strive to achieve *both* inner fulfillment *and* financial stability by creating their own work;
- how *our mind's "elevated" faculties* (e.g., strategic insight; spiritual and inventive intelligence; ability to "figure out" answers or take risks effectively) are *requisite vocational companions* in uncharted, uncertain times.

This book is for all who want to create their best vocational options and who may not know "how" to make the transition into work they prefer. It's also for the growing number of displaced workers and retirees who wish to *use* today's opportunities for novelty and lack of conventional job security to make their mark and contribution in the world.

Our planet is swiftly altering its geopolitical and economic boundaries. Everything seems in flux. Social values—how we work and live—fluctuate along with the value of the yen, the dollar, and the deutsche mark. Our notions of what it means to love, to marry, to be a parent, an employee, and to grow old are being debated and reexamined. Superfluidity now affects each of our lives.

The newspapers report that huge numbers of Americans now expect the government to create new jobs for them. At best this is simply wishful thinking. Even if realistic, by definition, the bulk of such jobs—such as summer employment for minimum-wage earners and teenagers—are short-lived and low-paying; they offer little security and even less fulfillment. This is not the sort of work I suggest you create unless it turns you on. Instead, I invite you to join our entrepreneurial era.

Today, concern over getting and keeping work is a national preoccupation.[1] Why then do some adults—the high-spirited few—feel so excited about their prospects for satisfaction and financial reward? Why do they sense opportunity in the very chaos others fear? I suggest that they've learned to exploit their circumstances, whatever these are, as leverage for what they want. They are entrepreneurs. Whether they work alone or for others or use temporary, shared, or part-time jobs to gain an occupational advantage, they behave *as if* they believe that they *can* structure a lifetime's worth of meaningful goals, tasks, and relationships.

We live in a "lesson world": Its problems can help us grow. Our desire to have someone else *give* us work, define our life's role, or tell us when and how to do things is an avoidance of the highest order—a obvious shirking of mature responsibility. Every generation has its share of hardships to surmount: One of our era's assignments is to manage tumultuous change. Another is to cultivate the highest self-awareness that transcends the idea that our good—and "the good life"—comes from without. I propose a radical, yet ancient, notion: To build the life you want—complete with inner satisfaction, personal meaning and rewards—*create* the work you love. By this I mean invent a way to earn an income doing what you do best, while serving others, becoming authentic, fulfilling the highest standards of your vocation. This is spiritual work. It's life's assignment. And most of us are well-equipped to do it.

# How to Read and Use This Book

In these pages you'll read about entrepreneurs of all ages and walks of life who, like my happiest letter writers, manage occupational change by creating their own opportunities. If tomorrow their ventures dried up and blew away, they'd invent meaningful substitutes. They have the self-confidence, skills, and knowledge to achieve what they genuinely want. Their stories are more than just entertaining. They reinforce enduring universal truths about human ingenuity and provide timely success models that illustrate how to become aligned with a self-affirming, spiritually aware life.

Stories can help you craft mental models of "how" to improve your lot in life. Stories have the power to raise your imaginative

I.Q. and to suggest ways to invest your talents and take control of occupational pursuits. I use stories positively to construct *encouraging* ideas: to build an edifice (or framework) of belief in the possibility of success.

If you're worried about your present job, if you can't find the job you need, if you believe in your limitations, what the doctor orders now are *positive* stories, success models, and the gaining of primarily mental tools to enhance—rather than crush—your emerging, creative spirit.

Walt Whitman's lines in *Leaves of Grass* remind us that we *ingest* stories—for good or bad—and are either nourished or depleted by the tales we eat:

> I understand the large heart of heroes . . . this I swallow, it tastes good, I like it well, it becomes mine . . .

You don't need more stories about dysfunction. And stay away from protective, too-explicit advice that actually erodes (rather than encourages) your ability to innovate. Believe this: No matter what your age or background, you were created for a purpose. You can discover and define that purpose in your own way. You *can* create viable, marketable forms by which to transmit your life's genuine purposes to others. If you think you *can't,* that's the belief or thought requiring correction: Find evidence of people who are doing what you want to do. "Swallowing" their stories will help to change your mind. Your beliefs can support, or snuff out, your life.

A publisher-entrepreneur I'll call Angela told me her father was a powerful role model. He helped her build a belief in the possibility of creating work. She learned from him that business success comes only with continuous effort. His lifelong efforts as a journalist provided a living example that taught her "how" to persevere:

> Every day I'd watch him slave away in our basement, polishing up his news items for eventual sale. He survived countless rejections. With stubborn persistence he'd write and sell. My

observations were like food. By a kind of osmosis, I learned to accomplish what he did and more. Now I find my own answers because of that childhood nourishment. Also, I tell my children that, although they crave easy, pat answers, accomplishment calls for independent thinking. Especially now.

It's been said that the best parents—and the most memorable teachers—encourage us not to lean on them, but to stand on our own two feet. This task begins in the mind. Angela endures her own career setbacks and rejections and credits her tenacity to her father's positive example. Since many of us don't have such examples, we must find role models wherever we can. Books, movies, or our own observations can aid us. The idea that you're always—and only—in business for yourself (no matter for whom you work or where) is one idea that helps you build entrepreneurial achievement. The idea that you can create your work (instead of merely *looking* for a job) is another. As you read my narrative and the success histories in this book, you'll find idea-seeds and inspiration encouraging you along the way.

# Work and Life Meaning

Some futurists predict that by the next century we'll live in a largely jobless society; there won't be enough employment to go around. Researchers point to robots and artificially intelligent computers already tackling the tedious or dangerous jobs humans *used* to perform. They tell us the rise of part-time and temporary employment and job sharing are but symptoms of this trend and that the only profitable corporations are those that downsize (i.e., terminate employees). I contend that even if finite, narrowly focused functions (done primarily for money) do grow scarce, an optimal life requires meaningful *vocation*—some active, contributive, relational work to help us become unique, whole persons. Until we achieve this integration, we have but half a life.

As we cultivate our talents and interests, we prosper—if "only" through keen, life-affirming enjoyment of each day's efforts, whatever these may be. We work for *more* than money although most people don't realize this. Presently, however, well-paying employment is still a survival necessity for practically everyone. This is debilitating, or else why do so many heart attacks occur early on Monday morning—just when people who'd rather be doing something else settle back into their compromising working routines. Although we may prefer to go fishing (instead of to our office cubicle), most of us must earn a living for decades longer than our forefathers simply because we are outliving them.

Work also involves relationships. Our achievement happens in the company of others. Not even the most solitary artists work solely for themselves. This explains in part why some people experience such bitter despair when lacking viable, appreciative outlets for their talents. (Here, creating options in a client base or audience can offer answers.) Whenever we revise our careers, our relationships change. One woman found that some of her friends couldn't stomach her decision to leave a status corporate job. They either dropped out of her life or became angry with her, even called her "crazy." Fortunately, her best friends were enchanted by her spunk:

> My oldest, closest companions share my adventure of altering priorities and lifestyle. They're challenged by my courage. We're now talking at a new, more intimate level.

Engaging and productive work stimulates sound mental health. But merely to be employed does not automatically mean to be "engaged." One man's extended depression lifted only upon leaving a spirit-draining job:

> I was despondent over continued corporate frustrations and visited a career counselor. In time, and with much support, I realized that, to the degree I took action on my values and needs (for me this turned out to be *relevant* work), my spirits

soared. This was my clearest affirmation that leaving my old job to create new options was right. Scary as it was, that single choice saved my life.

Be assured that my notions about these vocational benefits—personal satisfaction; enhanced relationships; meaning; our full engagement with contributive, productive tasks; the *potential* for financial security—are grounded in my life's experience. I write not from an academician's ivory tower, but as one who has corrected her own beliefs about self and work. By tuning in to *my* vocation, I've found material success and personal satisfaction.

# Divine Discontent

Toward the end of my tenure in public-sector educational administration, I felt strangely restless—what Emerson called "divine discontent"—and craved wider responsibilities: I experienced that boredom born of the need to give up what's called "the lesser self" and to grow into larger capacities.*

I'd learned just about all that challenged me from my various managerial positions and hungered for new lessons. In the early 1970s, I toyed with the idea of entrepreneurship as a critical *life-skill* because I was wrestling with my own limits. I wanted to *create* my own work as I might a sculpture or a weaving.[2] I saw entrepreneurship as practical—not some abstract concept for business school graduates or venture capitalists.

Personally, I felt my working life was too narrow. Daily my

---

*To be sure, there are other kinds of discontent, for instance, that mischievous boredom signaling inattention. Then we need to *stick* with what we're doing. Here we press forth. We discipline ourselves; we transcend the erroneous blocks we ourselves construct to thwart full engagement with tasks or others. But this is another matter to which I return later.

vitality drained. I yearned for *more*—more life, more creative freedoms, more energy. With these, I felt I could revise my options or reinvent myself—as I'd done spontaneously when a curious, adventurous youngster.

Maybe this narrowing of life—the eroding of interest and hope—could be likened to being cooped up in a room that's too small. You notice, perhaps for the first time, that you own a large property. You acknowledge you have sufficient resources to expand: money, room to grow, a vision of what you'd prefer. You wonder why you don't just knock out that wall, enlarge your little room, or even entirely remodel your whole house. What stops you? Finally the truth hits: The only thing that's stopping you is *you*.

At least that's how it was for me. I realized *I* was the only one blocking my approach to the grand dreams of my authentic life. By moving on, by handling my fears, by investing in my own God-given talents, I embraced a keen desire for personal and professional growth. I *knew* that if I stayed faithful to my aspirations, I would create my own niche. This, then, is one purpose served by our healthiest drives: to *force* us to use our talents.

Lest anyone think that I just jumped impulsively into a new career, be assured I took my sweet time. I spent *years* preparing—emotionally and financially—for leaving my public-sector job, although it may have appeared to colleagues that I moved quickly because I kept my plans to myself. Eventually, I positioned myself for launching the corporate and publishing projects I now undertake.

In the beginning, all was apprehension, confusion, delay. Gaining specialized knowledge, a tactical plan, accumulating money to finance my transition—these were the easier hurdles to jump. My toughest barrier was overcoming fear. I lacked courage to sever certain key attachments: a known way of life; social ties; financial security; a place of belonging within the trusted, respected community of my fellows. "Letting go" was a poignant, bittersweet task. I looked back with love, and ahead with excitement and equal mixtures of fear and faith. Personal experi-

ence tells me entrepreneurial growth—moving on—requires forti-
tude, lucidity, and emotional balance. You'll need lots of horse
sense. One thing is certain: Your self-beliefs either support or
undermine you.

## Follow the High-Spirited Few

There are always those high-spirited few who are challenged by the
prospect of meeting the unexpected crisis or joblessness. They
believe, "I'm the kind of person who can figure out what to do."
The best are at one with their vocations—they embody their work
and grow because of it. They are totally engaged with *whatever*
they're doing. They *like* testing themselves and believe in the
availability of their own answers. They take well-calculated risks
and instinctively understand what I mean by "creating work."

I hope to inspire and increase the acceptance of such attitudes so
that many more people learn to operate smoothly in our uncertain
era. This is the best mental health insurance for the millions who
feel depressed or anxious about their work, or who must manage
the stresses of ambiguity and the discomfort of existing in a
"no-blueprints, no-formulas, no-guarantee" workplace. (Note that
Americans now spend $12.4 billion annually to treat clinical
depression.)

If we require too much reassurance, specific direction, or
excessive hand-holding during today's world of abrupt transitions
can be unfriendly. This sounds harsh, but—like the Law of
Gravity—it's simply what is.

## How This Book Is Organized

I find myself writing this book with two voices: One seems
to encourage, perhaps persuade; the other is stern and prizes
self-discipline. I believe nearly everyone has special talents

and can *learn* how to earn money by using them. (Remember, I'm a teacher by trade and temperament.) On the other hand, skill, resourcefulness, and self-reliance are musts. I caution all to give up wishful thinking and dependencies, to stop hoping that Big Parent Business (or Government) will assume responsibility for our individual well-being. With my more severe voice, I urge you to take the time and trouble to identify and cultivate your inner gifts—within the explicit framework of your present circumstances. Invest in study. Locate good, reliable educators and counselors. Find your life's genuine meanings and use all the entrepreneurial prowess you can muster to express them. These preliminaries for change are an "inside job." That's why I dwell on the psychology and spirituality of entrepreneuring and offer inspiring stories of ordinary people who have tackled this successfully.

Chapter One suggests that creating work involves both short- *and* long-term innovation. Chapters Two and Three talk about *authentic focus*—your ability to heed and actively invest yourself in work that matters to you personally. Whatever you focus on, you attract. Chapter Four considers resourceful problem-solving skills and explains why you must be willing to experiment liberally and learn from your mistakes *before* trying to create work, "do what you love," or even express yourself effectively in your current positions. Chapter Five discusses risk-taking skills and provides you with some assessment tools (what's now popularly called a "reality check"). Chapter Six warns you to remember the much neglected art of strategic planning; this set of skills is a peerless asset to business success. It too flows from our inmost creative depths. And finally, Chapter Seven explores the mysteriously spiritual dimension of work, proposing that you can use work to develop your fullest humanity.

Throughout this book, I deal with the *process,* or life movement, of highly resourceful people. I hope you'll study their inner stance or thinking style (*not* just the "form" of their solutions) to reclaim your own ingenuity. Each chapter restates one certainty of existence: There are no guarantees.

The high-spirited few—people who *do* create their work and somehow do profit from it both psychically and materially—share seven attributes. These are substantive enough to govern beliefs, behaviors, and a unique worldview. Entrepreneurs are people of all ages, backgrounds, and temperaments, with all kinds of talents and dreams, who possess . . .

- *an inventive inclination,*
- *authentic focus,*
- *meaningful purposes,*
- *"figuring-out" skills,*
- *risk-taking effectiveness,*
- *a strategic, long-term outlook,*
- *high spiritual intelligence.*

Fortunately, each of these attributes can be developed. A graduate student of mine once likened entrepreneurial giftedness to piano playing. He said, "I can play the piano, because my parents forced me to practice when I was a kid. But I marvel at those who never had a lesson and play beautifully. Now that's talent!" I'll describe people who "play beautifully, *without lessons*" as well as those who are practicing to be entrepreneurs because their circumstances force them to.

Each chapter emphasizes one of these seven inclinations, while necessarily weaving the others into its discussion. By this book's end, I hope you'll have a textured, reinforced fabric of the entrepreneurial mind-set. You'll see that to the degree you cultivate vocational maturity, your skills will ripen and grow. Exercises throughout provide journal and/or study-group questions to help you integrate these ideas.

# The Three Stages of Vocational Awareness ©

## BEING

(unitive consciousness)
- Vocationally integrated
- Views work as "gift-of-self"
- Self-actualizing and inner directed
- Capable of giving and receiving
- Radical, direct experience of Reality, here-and-now, eat . . .

## SEARCHING

(advanced)
- Discovery

(intermediate)
- Exploration
- Seeks Meaning

(beginning quest)
- Loss of Meaning

## SURVIVING

(advanced)
- Counterfeit Achievement

(beginning)
- Survival

## SELF-ACTUALIZATION NEEDS

- Embodies own vocational values, skills, and "mind"; (I AM a writer, realtor, artist, adviser, etc.).
- Stewardship pattern: merges self and others' interests; cares for greater good; non-exploitative behavior, etc.
- Feels: "I was born to be, do this"; "I'm becoming my best, comprehending the world through this"; "I can't believe they're paying me to do this . . ."
- Embodies Maslow's "Being Values": joy, creativity, courage, truth, etc.
- Believes, "What I want to achieve is possible for me."
- Able to ask for what one wants.
- "Beliefs" dissolve in direct, full-knowing of who one is; transcendent or peak experience, etc.

## EGO SELF-ESTEEM NEEDS

- Excited Trepidation: "Is this possible for me? Can I do it? Do I dare?"
- Finds fit between authentic interests/purposes and needs/wants of others; "sees emerging pattern of vocation."
- "Anxious Search": study, purposeful research; fruitful use of holidays, time off, weekends; responsible, embraces serious inner work; raises information level about what's possible for self; engages in long-term strategic planning.
- "Divine Dissatisfaction": Feels restless, shifts of loyalty; stalls—feels life's on hold; reading and daydreaming increases; fears intensify; increased mood swings and/or depression; angered at not knowing; frustrated with those who can't/won't give specific, concrete "how-to" advice.

## SURVIVAL-SECURITY/SAFETY NEEDS

- Ego and/or money, status, approval, prestige driven; fear, greed, rage motivated; workaholism; outer-directed; may want something-for-nothing.
- Fear, anxiety, low self-esteem; inept and ineffective; dependency driven; dysfunction abounds; swings from "I'll make it no matter what" to "What's to become of me?"

NOTE: Juxtaposing an adaptation of Maslow's familiar "Hierarchy of Needs" against this chart, we see, once again, that more complex psycho-social values surface as lesser needs are met.

If I have ignored some significant aspect of entrepreneurial skill—such as the obvious importance of high self-esteem to fruitful problem-solving—it is primarily because I have already devoted whole books (or whole chapters of books) to such topics.

## Plan for the Long Haul

You'll probably support your creative venture for years—as loving parents support their young. Endurance generally comes by degrees, as you put one unsure foot in front of the other and, step by apprehensive step, learn to utilize your latent powers. You *can* sustain the tension of not knowing *exactly* what to do. You *can* find your own answers. It just takes time, patience, and letting go of illusory, dependent ways of being.

If we observe our era's decomposing mega-industries, its revolutionary global shifts, and its widespread, social, political, and economic uncertainty, we realize that mastering wholly new personal skills is now our number-one priority. As we move away from our erroneous "I can't" beliefs, as we build solid faith that we have within us the availability of answers or guidance, we establish the mind-set needed for life's true purposes. The matter of building a life (and a life's work) is, at heart, a highly spiritual notion, as well as an entrepreneurial one. Here's where educators, business executives, counselors of all sorts, and the clergy must join hands.

Our new job security comes primarily through a shift in consciousness. Figuring out the answers yourself when you don't know what to do is one key to entrepreneurial survival. Working with disciplined passion is another. Learning to trust your best instincts—what most of us commonly call a "gut feeling"—is a third. These aspects of personal resourcefulness are some of what we each can, and must, learn to build a fulfilling life. Our personal and professional success depends on it. To paraphrase Victor Hugo, entrepreneurship is a powerful idea whose time has come.

# CHAPTER 1

# An Inventive Inclination

> *To create work, we must cross over a threshold of*
> *inner development; consciousness is our doorway*
> *to the answers we want—we need enough*
> *creative depth to support our ambitions, to*
> *intuit, "This is what I must do" and to reason*
> *our way along.*

Your entrepreneurial future rests in the heart of your urgent needs. Think about it: Why did you pick up this book? What are you searching for? Do you want to be, or do, something new? Are you carrying a weighty personal or financial burden on your shoulders? That seems the case for around nine million adults, presently unemployed. Is your company laying off employees as an estimated 85 percent of United States corporations either plan to do or already have done? Are you merely bored and eager to exchange your conventional nine-to-five job for something daring? Perhaps you're one of the hundreds of thousands of displaced middle managers involved with an out-placement firm, secretly resentful that they're not finding a job *for* you.

Whatever your concern, your best life rests in your ability to find a fit between what *you* need and what others want. Fulfillment and money (in larger or lesser degrees) are by-products of this fit. To build the life you want, find that fit. It involves exploring both your limits *and* your passions. When you become intimately, *positively* engaged with your pressing needs, solutions crop up that you never before considered. A mechanical engineer marveled at this truth:

> Necessity is my best friend. When I'm really up against the wall, I'm forced to delve deep into my possibilities of choice. Then some new answer—usually one I least expect—flashes into my mind and saves me.

Let me caution you up front: I don't have pat answers or a linear, step-by-step formula for you to follow. What I do have is a wealth of experience, information, success skills, and anecdotes, and an educator's intoxicating desire to teach the interested—just like you?—how to find their way when they feel lost.

All my professional life (since the late 1960s), I've taught, coached, and counseled persons of all ages to *draw out* and productively use their inherent wisdoms and talents. This entails reminding almost everyone that they already *possess* a source for anything they could possibly want. The life we yearn for resides within. Scripture calls this an "inner kingdom." You might think of it as consciousness or your deepest mind. Your mind was meant to create—invent—the things you need and want. Serious achievers in every field stay in constant, intimate contact with this power.

Since 1980 I've been a confidential adviser to gifted, senior-level business leaders. Most are natural entrepreneurs—world-class thinkers—who routinely extemporize solutions to an unending succession of novel dilemmas in their business operations. This is what they're trained and paid to do—and what they love doing. Similarly, I'm retained to contribute to their nonstop, creatively productive flow. The skills we jointly apply flow from within to without. They are learnable—even transferable. For instance, many of my favorite clients have, upon occasion, lost their jobs as a result of surprise mergers, political realignments, or a sudden fall from management's grace. Invariably, I've seen them land on their feet in another, brighter spot. As the Introduction states, I've done the same. I've also observed the identical, *creative-adaptability* in people who lack a formal education or credible work experience. Each is a gifted entrepreneur. As the chart on page 14 illustrates (and as this and later chapters discuss), this means he or she *embodies* the very spirit of the function being served, and continually works to satisfy certain emotional or economic deficits while persevering resourcefully toward long-term life goals.

This embodiment, this "being-the-work," is why, at the third and most mature stage of vocational development, income is almost irrelevant. While people in the mid-levels of vocational development search for "meaningful" work, still debate this or that budgeting ploy, or try to calibrate how much they'll earn at this or that occupation, and while those at the survival levels grasp at any available job, the vocationally maturing seem more engrossed with the *spirit* of their work (with its craft, its poetry, its mastery) than with money, per se. Naturally, like learning to read, all this is a progressive phenomenon. Some comprehend more quickly than others. I sense the "swift" possess unitive consciousness—a boundless, creatively powerful mind.[1]

By their way of being, thinking, and behaving, the vocationally integrated carve out an enviable place for themselves in the workplace. Some work alone; others work in corporations. Some earn great sums; others less. But each innovates, strategizes, and experiments freely. They may *wish* for good luck, but they don't employ "magical thinking" to fulfill their aims. Hard work, superior judgment—often gained by using errors or setbacks—and creative energies move them forward. Each has impressive stores of a mysterious, life-affirming power that furthers selfhood and is totally unrelated to business. Yet somehow this power incomprehensibly forwards the successes of every venture. In large measure, it is spiritual—a transcendent mode of consciousness, nondualistic and liberated. Today, businesses fail when their leaders and workers lack this high-level awareness—a timeless mind.

Alexander Graham Bell said, "What this power is, I cannot say; all I know is that it exists and it becomes available only when [a person] is in that state of mind in which he knows exactly what he wants and is fully determined not to quit until he finds it." Lest this "something" sound like mere brute force or a Victorian form of willpower, be assured it is much, much more. This trait emerges from the vital integration of all our most human faculties: mind, heart, and will. Our deepest consciousness lets us think and act ingeniously, take control of our lives—both in and out of business. I call this *personal entrepreneurship*. For simplicity's sake, I'll use the word *entrepreneur*. However, I mean something far more exciting than either the dictionary or common usage suggests.

# Don's Story

Let Don's experience start my exploration of the entrepreneur's mind. Don left his parents' home when very young. He moved to a small country town and supported himself as a logger. While still only in his twenties, he realized he needed another livelihood. Don knew he'd have to transcend the traditional job seeker's mind, given his background. With self-inquiry and over time, he "invented" an answer:

> It struck me that with my knowledge of logging I could provide a tree-cutting service to my community and also earn a decent living as a chimney sweep. I wanted to work for myself. I've been on my own for so long, and am so independent, that running my own business seemed natural. Without any experience, I started my company part-time, working alone.
>
> I attended chimney-sweeping school for one week. Then I just placed an ad in the local paper and began. It took me about one year, part-time, to build my company.

*New Webster's Dictionary* states an entrepreneur is "one who organizes, manages, and assumes the risks of business."[2] This framework hardly suits our era, which begs us to become improvisers and innovators in all walks of life. As parents, teachers, community leaders, and teenagers—regardless of our age or everyday roles—we all need entrepreneurial skill. Fortunately, it can be developed—and not necessarily in a classroom.

A young woman wrote to me after she finished reading about right livelihood. She expressed a big entrepreneurial dream:

> I'm currently involved in a very unpleasant divorce. I'm trying to develop a way of working at home so that I can keep my ten-month-old baby with me. She deserves to be raised by her parent, not by a stand-in like day care or a baby-sitter.
>
> This is a totally new idea for me, one that's still sinking in and percolating around in my head as I reorganize some old ways of thinking and acting.

This insightful person is not alone. Most of us are "percolating new ideas, reorganizing our ways of thinking and acting," in part because of the incredible uncertainty of our times. Like Don, we too may have to transcend our old, job seeker's mind. For instance, according to a recent *U.S. News & World Report*, 60 percent of Americans believe our economy is teeter-tottering between "stagnation, recession, and a depression," and only 11 percent express "a lot of confidence in the government to efficiently solve [our problems]."[3] Our collective *belief* is part of the problem. Most of us want control over our work. We want to be creative. We *all* want liberty, joy, and rich fulfillment. These desires drive every wholesomely directed human. Intuitively, we sense there's a way out of our problems, but today's harsh realities (especially so for those who need a job) cause us to abandon our creative intuitions and instead give in to worries.

# Job Hunting Is Passé

It is no longer practical to simply *hunt* for a job. This is the quickest way to madness anyone could imagine. Our entire employment and hiring process, worldwide, is ripe for overhaul. High school and college graduates understand this intuitively. Young people admit feeling pessimistic about their futures: Information from newspapers, TV, the experience of friends make this the first generation of Americans who don't believe they'll live as well as their parents.

Added to youth's bleak view of the future is the cheerless state of approximately one million adults (all former job seekers) who have stopped trying to find jobs. In the 1990s, corporate America began reducing its ranks by approximately 1,500 jobs per day. Currently, only 15 percent of displaced workers can expect to be rehired. It's become apparent that for corporations to maintain fiscal integrity, they must continue restructuring—downsizing, trimming both middle management and blue collar ranks. Many unemployed now apparently feel too discouraged to go "looking for jobs." Who could blame them? Most human beings can take only so much rejection before giving up, especially when they don't really *want* what they're looking for.

Ideally, what we want is not simply a job, but to discover our life's *vocation*. A mere bill-paying job offers little genuine, intrinsic reward. True, a "mere bill-paying job" is fine if it supports our real purposes as parents, artists, or hospital volunteers. But after we meet our security needs with a "mere bill-paying job," almost all of us begin dreaming of our vocation—even when we don't really know what it is—because a *vocation* is *our deepest summons to be human in a particular way.* Sometimes we'll spend years preparing ourselves for a vocation while income is delayed. Or we must build a track record for ourselves before earning sufficient sums from our labors. This too is natural. Then we'll have to support our livelihood for decades. Most visual artists, actors, and others in the arts or in esoteric, specialized jobs work at other part-time occupations just for the privilege of doing what they love. (That's another reason why income seems almost irrelevant at the upper levels of human development.)

A graduate student needed money for tuition and books. He realized that he had, erroneously, learned to wait for someone else to tell him what to do. In the past his parents, teachers, or the managers at his various part-time jobs had been only too eager to direct his every step. They advised him what educational choices to make, guided his studies, and gave him marching orders for "how" to do most everything—find a job; do a job; act, talk, dress, and think when on the job. Observing these mentors, he sensed their lives lacked fulfillment and decided, *"I need to figure out what I want."* So he devised a way to adopt the *mind* of those he admired. He asked himself:

· *What are the thought processes of the successful people I most admire?*

This exercise led him to read numerous biographies. In short order, he probed his inquiry more deeply:

· *What's my major need and interest?*

· *Who else shares these?*

· *What might I do to serve them?*

Soon, he gathered a few likeminded classmates and began a study group to help stimulate everyone's creative juices.

You, too, can mull over these sorts of open-ended questions. To find your best answers—for either the short or long haul—don't push yourself for answers or worry about "how" you'll do things. *Describe the territory you want to enter.* Then, examine your anxiety level. Do you believe you can carve out a niche for yourself in that working world? Are you suddenly so excited about your future that you can hardly sit still? Do you experience mood swings or resentment because all this is so ambiguous? Do you feel angry or depressed because you *can't* invent (or answer) questions like the graduate student did? Control your emotions and read on.

Change can either challenge or threaten us. Use this book (and others) to raise your awareness about what *you* need. Hear what you say to, and about, yourself within your deepest mind. Your beliefs pave your way to success or block you. By spotting desirable options, by resourcefully retraining ourselves and by creating our work, hope returns.

We all chip away at this—at our dreams, ambitions, and our longing to be robustly whole. We may support ourselves with temporary or unsuitable jobs to pay our bills. Once we identify what we're after, we can tolerate almost any position. Treading these necessary, if troublesome, waters is just a way of moving ahead, toward our best options.

We may *have* to proceed conservatively, in an incremental fashion. Uncertainty and the scarcity of traditional work could well require this. The conventional job market offers dim prospects for finding (or keeping) jobs. Small- and medium-size companies are much more promising—especially for the resourceful, the highly skilled, and those well trained in sophisticated technologies.

## National and Personal Survival Skills

In one critique of U.S. industry, a prosperous European suggested that Americans have good ideas but lack the ability to "turn good ideas into good products . . . the Japanese and the Germans have been better [at that], faster, with a better quality and with a lower price sometimes."[4] This sort of remark was unheard of two decades ago. Only the inventive will correct deficits.

Whether corporate employees or proprietors of our own firms, we each must develop entrepreneurial skill. This requires a novel way of thinking that is creative and more independently resourceful than, say, the traditional work style of big corporate employment. To develop, we'll return to college or experiment slowly— on our own—or encourage our corporate and community leaders to invest in the finest educational apprenticeship programs and advanced, on-site industrial universities. Remember, to climb a profitable career ladder today, you need to spot options or create them. That's entrepreneurial.

Currently, 101 million Americans (or 55 percent of the adult population) shop from their homes rather than by going out to stores. I write this chapter amid forecasts that electronic retailing giants and "information superhighways" are destined to upset traditional retailing, learning, communication, and entertainment patterns. Here, then, are a few new arenas in which you could create novel services or products.

Then consider health care: Think *alternative* services and holistic products. Presently, 10 *million* adults pay—out of their own pockets, no less—for alternative medical care. Combined with the runaway growth of newly integrated fields of media, electronics, and computer technology, this melding of industries offers additional dynamic potential for handsome earnings.

It is decidedly *not* my intent to list our decade's brightest business opportunities. I only wanted to say if one learns to spot (or create) options, it's easy to get excited about the future.

Entrepreneurs imagine themselves eventually doing what they love or living where they want. They *believe* they'll gain control over their lives and build personal mastery by inventing answers to solve their own and *other* people's problems. A guaranteed salary and health-care benefits (like paid sick leave or vacation) aren't automatically included in their "create work" equation. The more self-actualizing the entrepreneur, the more they consider such trade-offs for entrepreneurial freedom fair and even *thrive* on figuring out how to pay their own way. "I'll buy my own health insurance," said one freelance secretary, "The freedom's worth it."* By contrast, those who can't see beyond today's survival needs may get angry or depressed. They worry, "Who will take care of me if I lose a job?" even as they complain about the job they have. Since I typically see the glass half full (not half empty), I write from my hopeful perspective.

To further your own dreams, it helps to study two types of entrepreneurs: larger-than-life heroes *and* average people. The superheroes are inspiring, to be sure. Yet when we hear that a young teenager, an ordinary displaced worker, or a seemingly hopeless, unemployed person has triumphed over some serious predicament, we're emboldened to reach out for what we want, too. We think, "Ah, if *they* did that, I can create something better for myself and those I love." For this reason, to promote my entrepreneuring-is-good message, I've interviewed individuals who have extraordinary courage as well as strong visioning and business execution skills. In most respects they are surprisingly like you and me.

## Barriers to Innovation

My interviews with those who improvise successfully reveal two well-known (well-guarded) secrets: First, almost all of us can do heroic things with our lives if we believe in ourselves and our goals. Second, most directions we need to actualize our goals are housed within ourselves.

To create work, we must cross over a threshold of inner development. Our entry point to the answers we want is *consciousness.* We need enough creative depth to support our ambitions, to intuit, "*This* is what I must do. . . ." It's been said that we are, do,

---

*This is indeed a risk. One could, conceivably, quit a secure well-paying job with fine benefits to invent work that's much loved only to be struck down by a grave illness. Alas, life offers no guarantees; hence we had best calculate our high risks carefully. (For more on high risks versus low, see chapter five.)

and have exactly what we believe we can be, do, and have. In other words, our awareness *is* our life. By cultivating it, by growing whole, we *hear* our best solutions—as if these were a radio station we are just now able to tune into.

My premise is that it's your *rounding out*—your robust, distinctive personhood—that fulfills you. Rounding yourself out as a complete person necessarily introduces you to your vocation. You admit your strengths. You start feeling "called" to do this or that project. Gradually that summons leads you another step until you discover your purposes. A vocation has transfiguring power: Daily efforts and relationships will become more truthful; you'll grow unimpaired and gain the practical know-how to *live out* your healthiest goals.

If you're like most people, you hold yourself back with three consistently, counterproductive habits:

1. *You distrust your inner wisdom and doubt that you possess an inventive inclination. (This renders you forever dependent on other people's thinking and advice.)*

2. *You lack a long-term plan or purpose and want your answers instantly, preferably in uncomplicated how-to "sound-bites." (Thus you stubbornly refuse to assume full responsibility for your own future.)*

3. *You undercut whatever positive glimmer of resourceful, long-term hope your* own *mind gives you about yourself and your circumstances.*

Almost all of us *fear* our potentials. We resist our truest, most genuine desires and avoid contacting the rich, wholesome depths of our own consciousness. One person fumbles (or side-steps) certain lucrative jobs that, over time, promise to yield his best returns. Another may reject hobbies or weekend avocations that seem odd to others. A third is apathetic. A fourth procrastinates endlessly. These are not "bad" people—just frightened and unfocused.

Generally, fear's message is that we're *not yet ready* to be, do, or have what we want. The way out of this dilemma is through a change of mind about *ourselves*—not simply the gaining of technical skills or textbook knowledge.

Fear is a natural, thoroughly human attribute. Initially, it simply tells us, "Pay attention!"[5] Sometimes we know full well what we're afraid of. But if we're crippled by fear, weighed down by a blanket of incomprehensible anxiety, then we can ask ourselves, "What do I fear losing?" This inquiry (especially when undertaken in the company of a competent counselor) usually brings bits of insight to the surface until, at last, we know.

In a counseling session, a bright and charming salesman confessed, "I don't think I have it in me to change." T. S. Eliot's lines, "It takes so many years / To learn that one is dead," reminds us what a breakthrough it can be to merely *notice* our delays, terrors, and secret demons. Fear blocks progress if we don't address it intelligently. Paying attention to our fear *feels* risky. At first, insights may make us edgy. Do we dare to take risks? Do we see an unattractive side of ourselves? Might we not yet *want* to take our next steps? We could uncover how stuck we are or discover something else unpalatable, perhaps something we *think* we can't handle.

## Entrepreneuring Brings, and Requires, Emotional Health

In this book as in my others, I assume that you, like most people, are well, not sick.* I'm writing for individuals who function, who love to learn and who are willing to develop twenty-first-century

---

*In using terms like "well" and "sick" I am, of course, referring to *emotional* health—not one's physical state—since some of our greatest creative contributors routinely inspire us despite their physical challenges.

skills. But even healthy, high-functioning persons grieve and feel low. Healthy people possess a dark side. They experience fear and failure, rejection and social embarrassment. They make mistakes and must learn from them. They are also soft and tender. They can be hurt (and regularly are) and easily hurt others. They feel all the painful emotions of "normal" life. Yet the emotionally healthy have several advantages: 1) They tend to be good diagnosticians. This is a key to their achievement edge. They know themselves well enough to rest when tired, to cry when hurt, to seek therapy when necessary. (Therapy seems in order for almost everyone at *various* crossroads, and certainly if we're in pain or habitually ineffectual.) 2) The emotionally healthy also recognize when enough rest, crying, or counseling is enough. By remaining ever alert to their subjective life—their inner goings-on—they actively participate in their healings, consciously electing the time to move on, to continue recovering and growing on their own. But some people may be too injured or too easily discouraged (or depressed) to build the skills described in these pages. Before you launch a business, you'd best be certain you have the soundness of mind and sanity to fulfill the job.

## Intuition Deepens

Your own animating essence stirs your desire to plumb your depths, live your truths, or solve money problems inventively. *Animating essence* is the spirit, the spirituality of full personhood. With self-development, intuitive powers strengthen. You sense the best direction for advancement or feel you can endure even when odds are against you. Someone's entire maturation process can be stimulated by loss, crisis, by physical pain or heartbreak, or by an ecstatic experience. No doubt you've lived through some trauma or miracle (a near-death experience; childbirth) that altered your life for the better. Initially you may have felt overwhelmed. (Chapter Two explores why such crisis points are often ideal opportunities for growth.) Whatever the stimulus, as you plumb your inner depths, you'll notice personal improvements—and not infrequently something akin to growing pains.

*Forbes* magazine featured a rousing story about Jack McWilliams, a cotton and dairy farmer. Some years back, McWilliams suffered such severe arthritis that he couldn't run his farm. In 1989, the bank was just about to foreclose on his farming property when, "in the nick of time," he recalled his grandmother's super health drink: a cure-all brew. "He spent about $400 on vinegar and juices, trying to come up with a mixture palatable enough to sell. After twelve months' work, he settled on a concoction of cider vinegar, grape juice and apple juice."[6]

Last year, McWilliams's firm sold $2.5 million worth of the tonic (called Jogging in a Jug) to stores around the country including Wal-Mart, Kroger, and Food Lion. Apparently, his most urgent problems, his physical and economic ills, jogged his inventive impulse and revealed his entrepreneurial hand.

# Pay "Positive" Attention to What Ails You

Another businessman needed to earn a higher salary. The thirty-something husband, father, and account executive didn't think that possible in his present job. He vacilated between quitting (to start his own business) and remaining in a secure job. I encouraged him to pay attention to what ailed him from a trust perspective—to mine the hidden gold within his own mind, to attend to *solutions* (what he wanted) rather than to problems (what he feared or didn't want) and to listen to his hunches for a few months before taking impulsive action. When he described himself as "confused," I suggested he think of himself as doing "research," that he start an idea notebook to clarify goals instead of dwelling on what he couldn't do. In a few weeks, he said,

I believed I was in an either/or situation—that I *had* to do this or that. But I've spotted at least three ways to augment my present income without quitting my secure job. Moreover, if anyone is receptive to creating alternative modes of working, it's my boss. I hadn't noticed that before.

This is what I mean by paying "positive attention" to what ails us: Rather than denying problems, focus inventively, intentionally, on what *solutions* might look or feel like. This is, in fact, how gifted scientists, entrepreneurs, and artists tend to invent answers. They continually tinker with possibilities—in mind—*before* taking action.

Our mind is *meant* to generate ideas that help us escape circumstantial traps—*if* we trust it to do so. Naturally, not all hunches are useful. But then you only need a single good idea to solve a problem. About this attention managing, one woman said, *"I almost feel the cells in my body becoming smarter."*

Along these lines, I heard one of my favorite success anecdotes when a woman phoned a radio talk show to share her story (which I'll paraphrase): Newly divorced, this single mother had trudged around town seeking employment. She couldn't quite translate years of homemaking experience into marketable skills—at least not adroitly enough to satisfy the officious personnel officers she encountered:

I waited and waited and waited in every personnel office while my application was scrutinized. No one hired me. The bill collectors were salivating at my door. I was just about to go on welfare when I had a brainstorm. I said to myself, "I know what I can do . . . I'm an expert at waiting!" So I took out an ad in my local paper. It read: "I WILL WAIT FOR YOU! Responsible party house-sits. I wait at your home for your delivery, telephone, or house-repair people while you go to work. $7.00/hr."

The first month she earned $1,200. The next, she made $1,500. By the third month, she realized, *"I'm an entrepreneur—I can accomplish anything I want."* Her comments underscore the lightening speed with which our finest insights solve problems creatively. At this very moment you may be just a shift-of-mind away from the answers you want most. Moreover, you need not devise a million-dollar business like Jack McWilliams. At the start, a modest community service enterprise could do you nicely.

Your entrepreneurial talents might find a variety of outlets: in a one-person business, in a tiny start-up company, in a corporation, or simply by reconciling some tough personal conflict. Maybe you'll start a crafts or catering company while remaining gainfully employed, full-time. Maybe you'll retire early and use your van to build a mobile pet-grooming service. Practically everyone needs a reliable handyman, an honest "domestic engineer," a green-thumbed gardener. Remember: Neither your entrepreneurial response nor your life is about style or form. It's about *artistry*. Your own transcendent thinking is what's needed first to lift you up—out of problems, per se—into what you now dream of as your "solution."

A solution-orientation is another primary advantage of every entrepreneur's mind. I'll repeat this frequently: *High-level awareness yields answers.* When solutions are what you need, when your well-being (or that of loved ones) is at stake, your intuitive powers are very likely to step up and come to your rescue. Sometimes, as mentioned at the outset, our darkest hours spark courage. This is what Steve Hui, founder of Everx Systems, Inc., calls "the refugee mentality": a pioneering set of attitudes, including self-discipline, sacrifice, a willingness to delay gratification that "rests, ultimately, on a fundamental belief that, in the end, one's circumstances are one's own responsibility."[7] Anyone—refugee or wealthy debutante—can use crisis to explore every avenue of escape. Intuition offers just one such avenue.

Twenty years ago, Dorothy Everett of Oakland, California, was a single mother of *nine* children, who desperately needed to find a way to support her family. She bet on herself, not an employment agency or corporation. With her background, she felt she'd never earn more than a minimum wage employed by someone else. Her mother had taught her, *"Work hard and you can get anything. Don't wait for someone to give it to you."*[8]

Everett (now 62) pinpointed her special talent: cooking. She borrowed $700 from a family friend and negotiated a credit line from her suppliers. Everett founded and built Everett and Jones Barbeque, a mini-empire of sauces and restaurants. Recalling that low point, daughter Shirley Everett-Dicko says, "It was hard . . . We gave up a lot—no vacations, no parties. We [worked] weekends, [stayed] open till five in the morning. We weren't happy then, but I'm partying now."[9]

Entrepreneurs like Dorothy Everett don't just take what the world deigns to grant them. They devise the means to have more—by translating their one-of-a-kind talents (or values or desires) into practical realities. Entrepreneurs breathe vigorous leadership into their goals. Dorothy Everett's "I can do this" outlook and honest self-assessment give her options, a reviving inner dynamism.

Instead of denying what ails you (e.g., fear, apprehension, limited education or means), *play* with the facts of your circumstances. Ask yourself:

- *What are my strengths?*
- *What would I advise a friend (or my child) if he or she were in my situation?*
- *What's my "I can" quotient? (Do I believe my goals are possible—for me?)*

Your continual awareness of possibilities amounts to "resting in solutions," as the sage Lao-tzu phrased it centuries ago. This is, at heart, the inventive inclination behind most creative choices. The effective entrepreneur incubates answers by getting absorbed in ideas, stories, news items, or even movies that illustrate the *spirit* of whatever it is they want. Many activities can promote such reveries about our goals. I've heard golfers and gardeners alike say their finest ideas come when they're looking the other way. Inventiveness is, in the final analysis, a highly idiosyncratic, spiritual process.

## Probe Your Inventiveness

Perhaps you don't view entrepreneurial achievement in this light. So, at the outset, let me reveal my bias: I believe each of us possesses a spark of divinity within. Intuition and inventiveness are simply integral aspects of this—an ally to success. All virtue, hope, cheerfulness, and *lasting* satisfaction are ours as we contact and use our life's inmost, animating powers. To assess your own inventiveness, ask yourself

- How hospitable to my mind's inner processes am I?
- What events or feelings prompt my daydreams, discontent, my desire, or need for personal advancement?
- How effectively do I play mentally with my goals? Can I *envision* my best future? Do I believe in that future?
- How much do I want independence (and all the responsibilities that word implies)?
- How open am I to my creative hunches or to those of others? (How many of my companions and close associates are inventive types? How comfortable am I around them? How do I treat my own intuitive promptings?)
- To what extent do I invest myself (time, money, efforts) in my own talents and good ideas?
- How serious am I about facing the challenges of my changing world or profession or in taking small, low-risk steps to escape my present dilemma?

• When faced with a setback or defeat, how (typically) do I care for myself so that I rebound with the energy, determination, or guts needed to move on?

Begin your investigation simply. Acknowledge your perhaps still-fragile impulse for growth. Admit your need for security or an interest you've been aching to explore. Mentally, toy with its fulfillment. What do your life's true attainments "look" like? Your own, playful mind can lead you out of ruts. One office manager said:

> When I started daydreaming about my future, I realized how indecisive I'd been. So I just played around with my work space, until it represented my new thinking process. As I moved books and files and cleared out clutter, my mind's eye started focusing: I got some great ideas for new projects. Life's restructuring starts simply.

It takes a relaxed, recreational imagination to coax insights out of hiding. To escape your seemingly limited circumstances, loosen up. Think smarter, not harder.

## Skillful Means and Street Smarts

In the words of one business woman, *"Entrepreneurs dare to live up to their potential."* Entrepreneurs design (at the very least, they *spot*) their best chances for work, self-expression, and authentic fulfill-ments. They take risks to bring their dreams to life. They invest in their talents shrewdly, slowly, lovingly. As a result when they're effective, they reap *huge* returns on their investment. Buddhists might call entrepreneurs people with "skillful means." Westerners would say they have street smarts or figuring-out skill.

About four years after Don started his chimney-sweeping

enterprise, an old back ailment recurred. He aggravated an injury sustained in his early logging days, while moving heavy cast-iron stoves. After deliberation, he decided to go back to college to study nursing. His own involvement with hospice care, before his brother's death, influenced his plans. Don's remarks reveal the *art*fulness of entrepreneurial thinking: Notice how he *instinctively* blends his heart-values with the practical necessities of everyday life.

> I'm interested in nursing because my little brother died of AIDS. He was a marathon runner, a scholarship winner, an exceptionally fine, pure person. He didn't drink. He never took drugs. When the quality of his life deteriorated, he killed himself. He was a highly effective man. I really loved him. During his illness I became a hospice volunteer.
>
> I worked with dying people on a limited basis, extending my support and friendship wherever I could. (This was even before my brother became ill.) The experience moved me to enter the health-care field when my back trouble returned.

Unlike most people (but exactly like Jack McWilliams and Dorothy Everett), Don didn't automatically adjust to or accept his limited prospects. He could have easily let his range of choices shrink. Instead, he creatively expanded his options, used his talents wisely, and developed his plans conservatively. Don took no unnecessary chances; he did take a calculated risk. Yet, as a result of his decision to change occupations, he improved the outcomes (both seen and unseen) of his entire life.

Returning to college, Don realized his primary asset was his resourcefulness. Other than sterling inner qualities, he had very little by way of savings. As you read this book, lack of finances or business connections may plague you as reasons for staying put. Similarly, the thought of letting go of a secure livelihood frightened Don:

As far as money goes, I've never had enough. This has been my main worry. But I put that down to my impoverished self-esteem. I've been so totally on my own, you see—there's no one in my family I could turn to, to ask for money if things didn't turn out. I didn't know how I'd support myself if my back injury worsened. So, for me, shifting careers was especially scary: I knew I had to make a change, but didn't know how I'd get the finances for school.

Don found his answer at the center of his need by examining, rather than denying, his fears. First, he entered therapy to improve his self-esteem and address some of the unfinished, injurious aspects of his childhood. Then he devised a long-term strategy: He'd sell his chimney-sweeping company to raise funds needed for full-time college attendance. Now Don brainstormed ways to supplement that income while studying:

I thought of starting a home-care, practical nursing service—part-time. My hospice training and college courses would help me train for this. I read an article in *Fortune* about a woman who suffered from muscular dystrophy, who also needed to support herself. She did well for herself with a practical nursing service. This is a service I can do without a heavy outlay of equipment, and it'll support me through school.

As I was completing this chapter, Don phoned to say that, for the third term, he's earned honors status in his course.

- I got my first, honest-to-God scholarship for next year. It's not much, but for a guy who couldn't even type when he left home, it's a major event. I'm thrilled with what's happening.

Despite crushing obstacles, or criticism, and all manner of financial and physical hardships, entrepreneurs like Don demonstrate how mental play—messing around with solutions—eventually yields answers. This truism applies to all kinds of endeavors: business, entertainment, politics, spiritual service, or a mom-and-pop store down the street.

Author Howard Rheingold defines the French term *bricoleur* as "a kind of intuitive technician who plays with concepts and objects in order to learn about them."[10] Some people dislike the fact that this thinking involves tinkering with the random materials at hand. They feel they're working on problems to no avail—that there must be a better method, a step-by-step formula perhaps that would work better than this "madness." In fact, the method of the *bricoleur* involves blending intuition and logic, awakening to factual elements of our answer we'd overlooked and noticing the nuances suggested by our "tinkering" as well. As we apply a heightened awareness to possible *solutions,* the variables of what we need somehow become more readily apparent. These yield the necessary data to take us a step forward. Either the situation changes, or we do. In other words, *something gives.*

## Benefits of Vocation

The best and happiest entrepreneurs approach both work and life as one seamless, fully integrated experience. This is right livelihood. It's also "vocation." These invite expression of one's highest values and intelligence in a progressively integrated fashion. Gifted entrepreneurs (like Dorothy Everett and Don) share many of these advantageous qualities:

- *They invest in their talents purposefully.* So absorbed are they in their projects and interests that they eventually lead the way, or influence others, or become known for their expertise, whatever the field.
- *They are effective risk-takers,* not merely by virtue of solid skills

and good judgment, but also because of their positive faith: What they yearn to accomplish or feel called to do, they're committed to. And, they don't shoot themselves in the foot with their risks.

- *Their belief systems and self-ideas (like self-esteem or self-confidence) support their life's objectives.* Underneath doubts, stronger than fear, lives the thought, "I can do this. I will do this. I am doing it!"
- *They manage their attention superbly:* We can think of this as having excellent "focus" or simply being single-minded.

# To Unleash Your Inventive Powers, Ask "What" —Not "How"

Can you vividly picture your goals? Inventiveness always asks that we form various ideas (however hazy) of *what* we want. Don't worry about "how" to get it. Here is where you may need to practice that random tinkering mentioned earlier: Manage your attention properly. Instead of automatically worrying about what you *don't* want (a thought train that exacerbates problems and compounds images of what you fear), become intensely involved with your solutions. I call this Positive Structuring. Your inventive inclination flows from the realization that your consciousness is the fertile, formless soil in which you sow "seeds" (in the form of ideas, mental pictures, etc.) of the fruit you desire. Your imagination is your faithful servant. Don't serve *it* by letting fear pictures control your emotions or your future. Employ your mind on your life's behalf. Having read thus far, determine for yourself how well you

- *Creatively maneuver around the obstacles of everyday life.*

- *Use your imaginative faculty as your faithful, most productive servant.*

· *Devise the mind, skillful means, and "street sense" to translate desires into practical answers.*

# Entrepreneurs Stick with Unappealing Tasks

At first, you may ask, "How can I imagine—or 'see'—what I don't understand?" It's *hard* to envision what is illusive—like answers. Yet, by sticking with the practice of imagining solutions, you teach your mind to persevere. Creating our own work requires us to *do* the work that we find most meaningful and rewarding. However, this does not mean doing only what we *feel* like doing. We have to be discerning about all this, mature enough to manage (or sometimes even to go against) our feelings and to be aware enough to know which feelings to obey.[11] You may *feel* like dwelling on your limits or fears. Don't do it. You may *feel* like sleeping late rather than getting up early for work, or *feel* like taking the day off (instead of sitting at a desk, phoning potential customers).* A perfect prescription for a squandered, unfulfilled life is to accommodate self-defeating feelings while undercutting your finest, most productive ones.

The form and process of invention varies from person to person. How we accomplish all this is art, not science. Your smallest task can be enabling, reveal larger challenges. Adopt this biblical precept: *"Be faithful in small, unimportant tasks; then larger ones will come your way."* Make this your life's operational rule. Observing your habits in small tasks trains your awareness—keeps you objectively awake. As you train yourself to stick with tough or unexciting projects or work toward distant objectives, you'll grow

---

*Then again, *some* unappealing tasks send us a signal that we should change directions. Here, too, intuition and figuring-out skills help us decipher what to do, when to do it, and when to quit. In any event, as Oscar Wilde pointed out, discontent is often a first-step of progress. Noticing it, we know *something* is amiss.

40

in self-mastery, even while tackling lesser jobs. This achievement alone elevates self-respect and optimism about what's possible. Meanwhile, keep pondering, *"What does my solution 'look' like?"* With faithfulness and personal ripening, you'll see your vision—or invent it.

## A SUMMARY STRATEGY

It has been said that the mind is a poor master but an excellent servant. Let your "servant" *invent* the future you want. Author J. H. Brennan put it this way, "The *vital secret* is this: Since imagination put your limitations up there in the first place, imagination is the thing to use to take them down again."[12]

Twenty-first-century realities demand new ideas—a *renewed* mind. "Set" your mind, much as you'd set a clock. Your old, immature mind demands, "Give me step-by-step directions. I need how-to advice." Your elevated awareness offers, *"Just describe the territory you want to enter; I'll help you live in your image of that land!"*

*Try This.*

In a journal (or to a trusted friend) describe your sense of what your *vocation* entails. Ask, "What would it mean for me to grow as a particular person?" or *"What* would it *feel* like to have what I want?" or *"What* might I do to prepare myself to receive that?" or "What do I long for?" Notice what images and feelings crop up as you ask yourself *"what"*—not "how."

- Envisioning *what* you need, what do you see? Use magazines, photographs, videos or movie images, if these are helpful. Pretend you "hear" a friend's voice tell you that your good has come about; *what* words, descriptors, and feelings are generated?

- Mentally describe your occupational goal in simple, positive terms: *Say what you want—not what you don't want* (e.g., "I want to earn money working at home, doing something I'm good at, that I enjoy" or, "I want to cultivate a positive, productive imagination").

- As you mentally play with the variables of your goal or solutions, *what* options pop up? Keep a scrapbook of ideas and review these frequently.

- *Pretend* you already have what you want. What do you "see"? When you were a child, you automatically used your mind to imagine a closet was a cave or that a broomstick was a horse. Children learn how to live in the world by rehearsing their future. They conceive of their "unimaginable" good by play-acting their way into their next levels of development and challenge. (Your positive imaginative power scans possibilities. Don't use it to think up more problems or ways to shoot yourself in the foot!)

*CHAPTER 2*

# Authentic Focus

> *You'll revive your powers as you revive your lost loves: your truest aims, values, and potentials; your feelings and most sacred realities.*

It's been said that before Bill Bowerman invented the airsole unit of Nike shoes, he asked himself, "What happens if I pour rubber into my waffle iron?" and that Fred Smith, the founder of Federal Express, wondered—and in fact wrote college papers about—what it would take to run a first-rate express transportation company using a hub-spoke concept. Albert Einstein pondered, "What would a light wave look like if someone was keeping pace with it?"[1] As a youngster surrounded by lovable but unhappy adults, I continually daydreamed, "What would it take to live a creative, optimally healthy life?"

Problems provide us with golden opportunities to create our work because needs hold our attention, and proper, fixed focus is required to find answers. When your rent is due and you lack funds to pay it, you're usually involved with your dilemma.

In fact, you *are* what you do with your attention. You gain dynamic personal power when passionately focused on your heartfelt objectives. You deplete your energy when you are worried or negatively engaged. This shouldn't need restating, yet it does. Most of us get seduced away from our intrinsic fascinations. We try to side-step our true nature, and this always results in unhappiness. The allure of money, the desire to earn approval, illusory notions about "success," the need to prove ourselves worthy to someone who may even discount our interests—all these, and more, cause self-abandonment. The flip side of this is that when we figure out what interests us, we tend to find our life's purpose. Entrepreneurs get lovingly absorbed with their problems and fascinations. Self-actualizing adults also tend to be highly motivated in their areas of interest. They *feel* loved, secure, rooted, and so they are able to turn their attention to tasks or some vocation outside themselves.[2]

# Focus Your Attention

If you attend primarily to what's worthwhile and desirable, you too can gain such power. To do this, you must manage your attention so that your self-sabotaging or negative feelings do not overwhelm you. The idea here is not to deny or ignore reality or problems, but somehow to resolve conflicts, and surmount obstacles while pressing forth. Determine your needs and values—not what you don't want or fear. Identify the mark you honestly want to hit. Know what charms you.

In our frenzied, uncertain world, it is the rare person who stays centered on what truly counts. If, as we create our work, we give inordinate consideration to our hindrances, if we agonize excessively about insecurities, money worries, or a futile attempt to please others, we erode our creative powers. By focusing on fears, resentments, or egoistic strivings, we give life to these personal demons. Our own attention energizes them. It's no trick to think positively when life runs smoothly; the time to manage our attention is when we need a job, feel anxious or rejected. Life's strict rule is this: *You get more of what you focus on.* Ignoring this, we abandon our healthiest, concentrative energies and court emotional upheaval.

Of course, it is completely human to dwell on problems or get distracted. This is why we are doubly rewarded when we single-mindedly pursue our authentic goals. First, a singular focus is grounding; we stay centered. Second, since interest and vocation are linked, an authentic focus helps us know what we really want to accomplish. When Isadora Duncan described her art, she said she had given her audiences "the most secret impulses of my soul."[3] Our truths—or authenticities—must be shared. That's the drive in our creative vision.

## Spinning Aimlessly or Regaining Focus?

Just as it's wise to hunt for a job when still employed, so is it essential to *focus on who we are at heart* even if we're not planning to become business owners. Corporate executives who know the unique value they're adding to their firms are purposeful. They project self-worth. Their company job does not give them identify or define them. One can sense they are their own persons— reliable, trustworthy, skillful. One woman began thinking of the advantages of self-created work only *after* she'd lost her job.

> I had been heavily identified with my nine-to-five position, and my job was so much a part of my life that I faced a giant identity crisis along with the job loss. I felt less of a person, less valuable. I felt frightened and angry. That's what got me thinking: How neat it would be to create my *own* work—if only in a scaled-down fashion and through my own efforts.

As I write these paragraphs, once expanding, prospering U.S. firms (e.g., AT&T, GM, IBM, Sears, UAL) systematically terminate employees by the thousands in an attempt to increase global viability. So-called downsizing has become synonymous with corporate profits. Yet rightly focused entrepreneurs find ways around such discouragements.

One business woman confided with frustration, "I've created the work I love, but the life I want still eludes me. I'm too busy, pulled apart in too many conflicting directions. When will balance and simplicity come?" My own experience says that, as with all human growth, shaping life toward the values or symmetries we favor happens over time, much like generations of evolvement—we notice improvements in say, seven- to ten-year increments. That's another reason why an authentic focus and meaningful purposes are so necessary. These encourage perserverance.

An editor recently told me she quit her secure publishing job holding one aim in mind: She wanted to write. Taking a cut in pay, she accepted a college instructorship—just to carve out writing time. Ironically, she'd have preferred to stay with her company, but they were inflexible about the hours. Keeping her sights on her true interest—writing—her mind was properly focused. She knew her worth and single-mindedly wrote her own ticket. An undivided, authentic focus orders our wits when all else is spinning about chaotically.

Without disciplining our attention, it's easy to lose track of who we are and forgo our dreams. Even people whose kindly, loving family says, "Do whatever makes you happy, dear," frequently can't find *what* they want until well into adulthood. Problems or a bleak economy then prod them to reconsider their goals and find their vocation. Your own crisis or the press of unexpressed talents may force you to locate your interests, too.

I didn't begin to find my way as an educator (or as a person) until two years after college graduation. I was so busy extricating myself from unproductive childhood circumstances that I brushed aside my innate talents. My early life was full of losses and uncertainty. Quite consciously, I prioritized certain tasks during adolescence: The first of these involved leaving an unsettling family situation. Thankfully, I put as much distance as possible between myself and disruptive conditions. As a result, young adulthood brought me much needed stability, allowed me to rediscover dreams I'd previously shelved. These put me back on track, and I invested in my talents, and gained confidence and resolve in the process. This is part of what it means to "build a life."

In graduate school, when I finally was secure enough to focus on my studies, I distinguished myself by willingly devoting myself to the disciplines of learning theory and human development. These were my real interests, and now I found it easy to study. Good grades seemed automatic. My old inquiry, *"What does it take to be optimally creative?"* returned to mind. Attuned to the summons of God-given gifts, I reorganized life effortlessly around themes and projects that enlivened me.

Similarly, your truths, talents, and *phases of growth* can rekindle that same absorbing, creative process. A first step is to build a secure base of some sort: within and without. Then explore what it means to *pay attention* to your truths, again inner and outer. Next, polish up the reverse side of this coin: Namely, relate your interests to *enduring life purposes,* your sense of destiny. Initially, ask yourself, *"What's worth doing?" "What attracts me?" "What makes me willing to stretch and struggle?"* Then tackle the long-term task of translating these inspirations into a vocation—what you do with your time and talents for yourself and others.

## Focus on Your Cycles of Growth

Life's ups and downs provide windows of opportunity to determine these values and goals. For example, during a crisis you may feel an urgency to sort out your directions. Grief or fear can *force* you to face what you've been avoiding: impoverished relationships, alienation from your own wisdoms or insights. Think of using all obstacles as stepping stones to build the life you want.

When Fernando Mateo (about whom you'll read more later) was only fifteen, he dropped out of high school. He knew school was not for him and wanted to learn a trade. His father paid him to learn the flooring and carpeting business. As a teenager, Mateo's authentic interest led him into business, and away from academics. Today, as president of Carpet Fashions (a multimillion-dollar carpet business in the Upper East Side of New York City), Mateo now teaches others to succeed.[4] I suspect strong leadership drives and an entrepreneurial bent were internal pressures he could not ignore. What internal pressures stir *you* to take risks or improve your life? Creating work requires active engagement with something worthwhile—of value to us and to others. Each of us needs suitable incentives to take us where we want to go; genuine interest is one.

Perhaps you've adopted a passive stance toward your work. You accept whatever jobs come along. Maybe you think primarily about income while ignoring your vocational preferences. Have years passed while you've slaved for material security and neglected loved ones? Possibly you've suppressed knowledge of what you love. Many people who talk of putting "balance" into life really want to spend time with their family. One man's financial setback afforded him a second chance at truth-telling. While laid low he reviewed his interests:

> I've been working through your book for ten months. There are days when I get drowsy with resistance. On other days I hurt badly. I'm grieving over an irretrievable past. But, as you suggested, I found an experienced counselor and have discovered what went wrong. Some twenty-five years ago, I abandoned my interest in human relations to forge a blazingly successful career in industry.
>
> After the recession hit, I lost my business. No one in my family discussed my loss (after all, they'd never spoken to me about business before). I suffered tremendous pain, but joined a career center and continued to explore. I've found a new world of ideas, ideals, challenges, and possibilities that I'll review for years. I'm now resolved never again to sell so much of my time and energy that I don't have enough of the same for my true goals.

Often, when corporate executives lose their jobs or promotions, their first reflex is to scurry right out and find any other (potentially oppressive) position. Their fragile, quick-trigger reaction deprives them of much-needed thinking time. Between our loss and our next steps exists a valuable *cycle for growth,* which we can use to identify our genuine interests or current needs. We abort this opportunity by rushing toward clichéd solutions. Here, too, we must appraise our own level of development: Are we sufficiently whole and thus *able* to explore our higher values and aims? Or, do we still experience reality in survival terms, struggling with fears or ineptitudes, or going-along-to-get-along? We can devise a personal strategy of entrepreneuring, wherever we find ourselves. However for fulfillment, practical achievement, and healthy growth, we must meet ourselves honestly—right where we are now.

One vivacious marketing executive landed a new, well-paying spot only *days* after leaving her old one. She didn't know it then, but she was growing, from the survival level to the seeker's level of vocational awareness. (See the chart on page 15.) Within a month at her new job she was depressed. Finally, she sought counseling and soon acknowledged that she'd sold herself short by focusing on her material needs and ignoring herself as a whole. Therapy helped her identify valid interests and learn to use her inner resources.

Sometimes severe disappointment or loss reveals us to ourselves. Finally, we admit what we've denied. Such was the case for Woody, a successful corporate engineer who rediscovered his love of carpentry only after his grandmother died:

> I was unhappy but didn't acknowledge it until my grandmother, whom I loved and greatly admired, visited us from Boston. She didn't say much, but I sensed her concern for my welfare. She saw how stressed I was.
>
> Five days after my grandmother returned to her home in Boston, she died. In settling her estate, I was shocked to find how small her income was. She was always so generous with gifts and money to all our family. Her death and her example were my awakening—the climax to my progressive dissatisfaction. This was my point-of-no-return for the life I now have. Still, I took months and months to make the transition.

Creating a vocation necessarily spans *decades* of existence. If, consciously, you're building an authentic life, you'll use every experience for your aims. You'll pass through any number of phases and crisis points, surprises and twists of direction. You can fold all these into your efforts to reach your long-range purposes, as Chapter Three discusses.

Then, too, your every advance in clarity or achievement may be followed by confusion. Growth itself introduces new problems and untried conditions. These cycles repeat endlessly. Each one offers us pieces of the puzzle that is ourself. We mature, we learn to persist, we build up wisdom and even profit from setbacks. After a while, words like "winning" and "losing" or "success" and "failure" cease to be relevant. We'll notice we're constructing a life—becoming an increasingly whole person faithful to our life's deepest, most productive themes.

## Stephan's Story

Stephan lives in California, in a small coastal town. For years he has held two jobs—as a newspaper printer and as the sole proprietor of a photography business. He loved photography even as a child when his mother, a photographer, encouraged his talents. Stephan was six or seven when he first got involved with cameras. But, after high school, he went on to other things and didn't touch a camera. For him, the period *away* from his passion invited significant growth. On some barely conscious level Stephan knew he needed a rich assortment of activities for his eventual vocation:

> That time [away from photography] taught me about life. I was a business major in college. Then I worked in every kind of job: as a mailman, a computer programmer, a salesman. All that experience was extremely important. A photographer needs a deep understanding of people and life to be any good

at all. And I sure learned. Anyway, in my mid-twenties, I left the city. This was a tough spot to be in at twenty-six. Here I was, in a small rural town, not knowing what to do with my life. I did odd jobs and sat around a lot, wondering what to do. It was rough.

This is an example of that unstructured meandering that Chapter One explored. Such cycles introduce the question, *"What's worth doing?"* As we grow toward full personhood, we try to answer honestly. Yet, so many seemingly successful business people cannot tolerate feelings of helplessness engendered by this reflection. They won't tackle the frustration of what they call "laziness" and fear wasting time. Yet a certain "laziness" actually *promotes* the creative process, even if, at first, we may feel disconnected from routines and structures of our usual life.

Creativity expert and author John Briggs compares creative laziness to the non-doing of contemplation rather than to the "idle hands" problem that threatened the Puritans. A bug-eyed, aggressive concentration (the linear-thinking, assembly-line sort that *must* always produce results) is not necessarily productive. Robotized people easily feel guilty about doing "nothing." They've learned to *do* anything compulsively, even trivial chores like mowing lawns or cleaning cupboards. Organized philosophies have taught them to suspect whatever doesn't lead to incessant productivity or concrete outcomes. I heard someone recently propose that all laziness is sinful—the devil's playground. One hardly knows how to respond to such archaic and punitive ideas. Even creative individuals employ this antiquated reasoning, but fortunately, their thinking usually goads them into that loving absorption required for substantive insight. Says Briggs:

> Feeling a constant need to jar themselves from their sulfuric laziness could be a way of forcing themselves to return again and again and again to the creative enterprise they are working on, keeping it always before them.[5]

When every hour and day of your life is scheduled tightly; when every ambition is prearranged by authority figures; when your speech, grooming, leisure pursuits, and values have been programmed by others, you need a hero's courage to face the anarchy that deep self-inquiry stirs up. Here's where professional support can help.

Stephan sustained months of uncertainty. During this period he met an ironworks sculptor who gave him an old camera. That reminded Stephan how much he loved photography:

> I realized then that my creative edge was in photography. (This was after I started taking pictures again every day.) I'd ventured into photography as an artist. I was happy and working. People were coming to me, buying my photographs, asking me to take pictures of all sorts of things: food, weddings, their portraits. Business skill came later. That was harder, even though I had a business background. There's such an enormous maze of paperwork. It takes a lot of self-discipline to bring the art and the practical business part together. This demands staying power and the right focus.

No sooner did Stephan decide to locate his photography business in a small country town (instead of in a well-populated urban area) than new worries washed over him. He admitted, "There was now so much to do, I didn't know where to start." Keep in mind that Stephan was motivated more by a *vocational call* than rudimentary, fear-driven worries. His choice to remain in a rural community was the harder, narrower way and represented values he wanted to be part and parcel of his existence:

> I felt that if I could earn a living here, as harsh as these conditions are, I could make it anywhere. This didn't make matters easier. If you start a business in a remote place like this, you need to gather all your forces—proper focus, wits, and courage—to keep it together.

Such "gathering of forces" requires a love of truth—not just comfort—and enduring personal power and tenacity. An authentic focus stimulates these forces, as well as imagination, intuition, hopeful energies, and ideas. As you become a full-fledged person, instead of minimizing or discounting your talents, you realize you *own* these resources and that, in fact, these contribute to your creative edge. Instead of fearing "laziness," you *use* it. Your gifts become your self-evident coin of trade in the world—the means whereby you gain not just monetary wealth but also altruistic or transpersonal pleasures.[6] We often hear much about the importance of perseverance, that without it, dreams are lost. Authentic focus seems the living fount from which characteristics like perseverance flow.

When you're psychically healthy enough to attend to what you love (or simply do well), it's natural to feel that you're spending your life's time and attention meaningfully, as you were meant to. Now, you have a positive expectancy about your future. You become *meta*motivated (or intensely turned on) to certain abstract values—like beauty or justice or some other esteemed quality. Authentic people are activated by their inner truths.

Stephan's relief (at rediscovering photography) is echoed by a former engineer who, after a brief stint in electronics, became an art teacher:

> I'm in my tenth year as a high-school art teacher and have many moments when I've looked heavenward even in class and thought, "God, take me now. I couldn't possibly be happier." Or, "Wow, I should be paying the school to do this." As a teacher, I've experienced both exceptionally foul and damning days and incredibly blissful ones, but I wouldn't trade any of these for the soulless, anxious, strictly-for-the-money existence I was leading.

Both Stephan and the art teacher demonstrate that intrinsic, focused passion fuels effort. They are, as it were, in love. Their loving absorption with their work and their innate talents draw forth meaning and pleasure. *Attention is power.* You attract what you focus on, so you'd best attend to who you are and what you truly value, or you'll get lots and lots of that which leaves you cold.

## Blocks to Authenticity

We begin to lose our passion in childhood. We quell our preferences, suffering progressive diminishing in the process. Maybe when we were "just ourselves," our parents, teachers, or siblings were jealous or discounting. Needing their love, we twisted ourselves into the more acceptable (but misshapen) forms we thought they preferred. Of course, in doing so, we erased *ourselves* from existence by suppressing our power, interests, and feelings. In due course, we forgot who we were and what we wanted to do with life. Too many of us have placed our trust in others who are abusive and then unwittingly accept their negative opinion about *ourselves.*[7,8].

You'll revive the power within your authenticity as you grow intimate with your lost loves: your truest aims, values, and potentials; your feelings and sacred realities.

Properly attended to, talents, hope, and energy return. You may actually *feel* rekindled optimism enabling you to persevere at boring part-time jobs (if that's required to make financial ends meet). Instinctively, you sense the logic to such cheerfulness, even if, at first, you don't know exactly what that is. One friend simply found she had a "glimpse of hope, an absolutely vivid sensation of joy—for no reason."

## Focus on Others as Mirrors

Others' absorption with what we're doing can give us clues about our "center of gravity." Generally, we hold another's attention when *we're* excited about what we're doing, but not when straining to fulfill tasks of counterfeit worth.

When Robin Helene Vogel was a child, her playmates loved her storytelling. A few years ago as a concerned parent, she realized how repetitive most children's entertainment is: "All the same clowns doing all the same magic tricks for all the same bored kids." She then remembered the rapt attention she attracted from her classmates and decided to translate her talents into a business she calls Travelling Storyteller. Now, several times a week, Vogel dresses up in a white evening gown and sparkling tiara to tell stories to "crowds of enraptured children" near her home in New York.[9]

Whatever your occupation, you'll capture your *and others'* appreciation when displaying your talents. It's generally a pleasure to watch people mindfully addressing their vocation. The growing popularity of sushi bars across the country testifies to this. Who isn't mesmerized by the deft chopping, slicing, cooking grace of the sushi chef? This seems sheer poetry in motion. The same seems true of professional athletes, dancers, even community leaders. We enjoy such performances, to the extent we're watching those who've mastered their attention. Consider the times *you've* been absorbed enough in a project, a presentation, or a sales pitch to stop being self-conscious. Magic happens when you fully attend to your task or to your customer's needs. Self-forgetfulness seems one hallmark of professionalism.

A genuine focus solves other problems, too. When farmer-turned-vinegar-king Jack McWilliams (mentioned earlier) needed a bottling company, he approached the chief operating officer of a private-label manufacturer. The subject of money surfaced, and it was obvious McWilliams had none. He offered to pay for the bottling with his last few bales of cotton. "As much touched as impressed," the CEO of the bottling company accepted the deal, then buried the paperwork.[10] When we're authentic, others usually perceive us as such and will often go to great lengths to help us succeed.

At nineteen, carpet company president Fernando Mateo required a line of credit he found almost impossible to get. His distributors wouldn't even speak to him. One day he vowed to himself that—by the end of the day—he'd have his line of credit:

> I said enough is enough. And I walked into this guy's office and I dropped down on my hands and knees and I said, "Please . . . give me an opportunity," I told him. "I will pay you back for whatever you give me on credit." And the guy said—he was shocked, you know—he said, "Get off the floor, kid, you're going to make it."[11]

Mateo got his credit line. When we're real, we're believable, credible. These profitable qualities flow from an authentic focus. These are also *spiritual* attributes that animate us from within.

## Focus on Your Energy

Think of your energy as fuel. What good is it to identify your fascinations and goals if you're too tired or stressed out to pursue them? By "focus on your energy," I mean take care of it so you can use it more effectively. The finest performers befriend their energies as one might another person. Consider Olympic athletes who demonstrate such grace under pressure. They condition themselves. Successful entrepreneurs, like champion athletes, know they must perform under pressure. Here, too, it's easier to manage energy (and stress) when we're at one with the life forces and truths alive in us.

My favorite "retired, grownup caddie"—Harvey Penick—offers this advice to those involved in special competitions (like creating work?):

> Be yourself. Do as you usually do . . . It is your mind that will have the most to do with how you play the big match. That's

why you should avoid new or different things that will distract your mind from your normal routine . . . Put the results of the big match out of your thoughts. [Those are] in the future. You want to stay in the present.[12]

How do you feel (and *behave*) when the stakes are high: right before a job interview, a public talk, or a prearranged confrontation? Does your body, your breath, and your emotional state advance, or undermine, your ability to think, speak, and function?

The most productive entrepreneurs I know *gain* energy by managing it. They may get a massage at noon, or work out in lieu of eating a heavy lunch. A pharmacist friend is a "fruitarian" as well as a fresh-air enthusiast. He runs miles each day. I've never known him to be sick (and none of his family goes to doctors either). He believes fruit sugars give him the mental clarity and physical stamina he needs to work a ten-hour day.

Physical workouts, massage, meditation, yoga, and proper diet (not necessarily limited to fruit) may well ease tension or rev up your creative thinking faculties. Aldous Huxley said his father considered a walk in nature like going to church. Instead of frittering away your vibrancy with worry or distraction, realize your mind and body are inextricably united. What calms and tones up one, soothes and improves the other.

You can start managing your energy wherever you are *now*. Consider having a planning meeting with your health care practitioner. Build on your existing strengths; move ahead only as inner and outer cues give you a go-ahead. If you're always sad, tired or irritable, visit your doctor. In terms of productivity alone, topnotch health is worth a fortune, since fatigue, unexpressed hostilities, and pressure play a large part in work-related illness. When you're well, you save money on medical bills; you have energy for your goals. Vitality also translates into widened opportunities: People *like* to be around us when we're centered and enthused. Moreover, sound health and relaxed, stress-free achievement go hand-in-hand.

One man planned a "voice-over" business (reading radio ads

and recording corporate training programs). But simple tension undermined his initial entrepreneuring moves. During auditions, extreme nervousness caused him to grow hoarse. He stumbled over his lines and generally became brittle when editors, producers, or engineers criticized him. In desperation, he devoted months to deep breathing and yoga exercises to get his mind and vocal chords under control. Only then did he land contracts. Similarly you could be waiting for "lucky breaks" that might come more quickly if you were simply calm and properly focused.

Think of this as training for an athletic event. Your basic, earliest preparation paves the way for your easier (perhaps amateur, or trial) events. As you build skill and confidence, as you get to know yourself—with practice—you may enter professional level events. Quite a few people even make it to the Olympics.

One young beautician's goal was to style the hair of affluent patrons. He felt he'd have to smooth out his rough edges first, so spent time and money refining himself. He needed to build comfort with the clients he hoped to serve. He took elocution lessons, prepared an outward "image" to conform with up-scale expectations and methodically readied himself, for the success he said he wanted.

By contrast, when a youthful sales agent met with initial customer resistance, her manager watched her become frustrated, then easily defeated. Each day, the novice salesperson quit and went home after hearing just a few rejections. Part of her self-conditioning involved practicing sustained confidence—even when prospective buyers said "No." Her manager coached, "Think of it as your job to be a 'no collector'—you'll need many rejections before closing one deal, so see how many no's you can gather." The ability to tolerate the discomfort of repeatedly hearing "No, thank you" involves building a thicker skin, lessening our egotistic need to succeed at every turn. This is strengthening ourselves where we're now weak.

A computer repairman told me that when his company fired nearly all its middle-managers, they kept him on the job.

I've made it my business to improve myself each year, to diversify my skills, to give customers *more* than they expect whenever possible. Going the extra mile routinely is a discipline for me—I wake up early each morning, sit in my garden with my coffee, and reflect on how I can better serve my customers. No one tells young people about this self-training, but that's what it takes to succeed.

Learning to work through pain is another aspect of self-training. An arthritic acquaintance worked through constant physical pain by training himself to think and behave as if he were robustly healthy. He once told me, "Conditioning is everything."

I've overcome extreme shyness and a fear of public speaking by "managing attention." My three-step long-term plan for this included study, practicing new skills, and methodically extinguishing the self-consciousness beneath such fears. Someone else may interpret the phrase "managing attention" as an edict to revamp their handling of everyday tension (e.g., learning to work for a hostile employer). Despite rejection, a family crisis, illness, or financial problems, we *can* function. To build a life we want, we need strength to grow beyond current obstacles or misery.

Moreover, self-training eventually makes us honor our obvious limits. Although it sounds paradoxical, in this matter I agree with Charlie Brown who once said, *"There is no problem so large that it can't be run away from."* It's unproductive, even toxic, to *force* ourselves to tackle totally foreign objectives. After all, why would anyone struggle and strain to create a counterfeit life—or a work they loathe?

This brings us back, full circle, to the matter of authenticities. To succeed in our venture, we'll have to *protect* our integrities—financial, emotional, and creative. For instance, I rarely answer my phone when I'm writing. I know managers who arrive at the office extra early—when no one else is around—to complete their most urgent projects. Others stay late for the same reason: to work when it's quiet and energy is at its peak. Managing energy frees us to attend to priorities. Mind, body, and superior productivity are one seamless, expressive whole. By managing energy we learn when our mind is sharpest, and guard ourselves from tiresome people, needless encroachments, and dispiriting ideas.

This entails moving beyond self-imposed boundaries such as what you fear or won't do or don't like. Much self-conditioning happens *first* through awareness. An example: To succeed financially, you'll probably broaden what you believe your mind, heart, and hands *can* do. Introverted entrepreneurs become at least marginally extroverted when their marketing and sales goals demand it; extroverts may appreciate (perhaps for the first time) the value of their early-morning or late-night solitude. We first must think "I can," then behave appropriately along that line of thought.

# Focus on Solutions

Those who dwell in solutions have a "21st Century Mind." They possess a cluster of skills that help them innovate. At the end of one of my lectures on this theme, an attendee rushed up to me excitedly. This mother of an eight-year-old said,

> My son is a born entrepreneur. He envisions the universe of what's possible before choosing and always sees "the lay of the land"—the big picture—when solving problems. Even at eight he likes to know his options before moving ahead. He has what you're calling a 21st Century Mind.

A former acquaintance simply "chews" on what she wants. This young wife and mother of two preschoolers (I'll call her Bess) was a cashier at the general store near my rural home. Bess is lively and good-natured. At this point in her life, her vocation appears to be parenting. Plus, she has numerous creative hobbies. Bess's husband, a repairman for a utility company, was scheduled to be relocated, and Bess was worried about the logistics of this transfer. The family needed her working income (from a part-time job) but because she was moving to a larger city, Bess didn't want to leave her children alone with a strange baby-sitter or in an unfamiliar preschool. She wanted flexible work, preferably a job that let her work at home. She spoke to me about this several times, and every time we talked, she seemed to be thinking out loud. I sensed Bess was incubating her best-case scenario by verbalizing and mentally playing with solutions.

One day when I went in to buy supplies, Bess greeted me radiantly. The day before she had made a discovery: She could turn her cake-decorating hobby into a home-based business.

> I applied for a part-time cashier's job at the local market [in the new location]. I'll work there when my husband is at home with the kids. However, immediately I'm going to create my own cake-decorating business. I'm good at this. It's fun. And, if I can grow this business, it will give me the extra money we need, and also let me stay home with my children for as long as I want.

## Authentic Solutions Serve Others

Entrepreneurs find ways to address others' needs and profit by also paying attention to their own. This isn't necessarily a sign of enlightenment or even high spirituality. It's just good sense. I read about one prospering fast-food business whose owners provide patrons with healthy, low-fat fare. The successful restaurateurs are two mature women with families. Before starting their company, they examined their own, hectic schedules to determine what services *they* needed. Always pressed for time, they realized when they traveled, it was impossible for them to eat sensibly. Their own life-style requirements shaped their business vision.

A San Francisco secretary opened her office-services business in her minivan, which she customized (and fully equipped with word-processing gear) to make "house calls." She captured customers who her competitors missed: people too harried or housebound to leave home. This solution won't occur to someone who doesn't empathize with others' time pressures. Another entrepreneur developed (and packaged) an at-home physical-fitness system. She's now expanding her personalized workout program by networking, by making on-site speeches at businesses, and by hiring other personal trainers to help the firm grow. When one man couldn't find a clean, affordable apartment, his predicament led him to create his present business: an apartment-finder's service. Here again is Chapter One's rule: Our needs hold entrepreneurial promise when we think inventively, from the vantage point of our and *others'* concerns.

By contrast, business persons with the old mind (I call it a 20th-Century Mind) envision only what's always been. They don't *try* to see the lay of the consumer's problematic land before choosing their options. If their company served larded-up sandwiches ten years ago, that's what they'll offer today and tomorrow, no matter whose arteries clog. If secretarial or fitness businesses have always settled in sterile office centers, that's where they'll put theirs, even if customers don't want to drive there anymore. What's tried and traditional is good; what's new is suspect or downright "bad."

Those with outdated minds decide in advance what they'll see and how they'll behave. Their "I should," "I must," "right/wrong" reasoning casts a restrictive, foggy spell over their imaginative faculties, clouds their visioning ability, and conceals the winning move they want. Eventually their own injunctions become rigid expectations for others. In time, they tell *you,* "You should/ shouldn't . . . ," "You must/mustn't . . ."

The Zen Buddhist saying, *"What you do, do that,"* is sublime advice for entrepreneurs. To create work and a life of your own, home in on and devote your energies and attention to whatever it is you're doing right now. Are you listening to the news while reading this book? Are you fretting about your health while doing the dishes? Try doing *one* thing to the best of your ability, and see how you feel.

If you "live" in your authentic solutions, you'll notice all sorts of ancillary answers, such as what consumers want globally, or what's happening to interest trends, or how the quality of your product compares with that of competitors. Put yourself in your client's shoes. Experiment with any known fragment of your answer.

## Vocation Deepens Authenticity

Entrepreneurs excite us when they're *authentic* in their success. Over time they do what they sense themselves *born* to do. It's *fun* to watch people becoming true to themselves. We see their old, job-seeking mind vanish (even if they work for others). A lawyer becomes a balloonist. A realtor starts a craft store. A teacher joins the Peace Corps. A physician begins a spiritual ministry. A homemaker studies accounting, then joins a prestigious CPA firm—or starts a cake-decorating business in her kitchen.

When an acquaintance discovered he was HIV positive, he became an entrepreneurial dynamo. He addressed his infection by starting a nonprofit foundation to debunk selected myths about AIDS—the chief one being that it can't be cured. To date he has reached 200,000 people with his message. He ran a Sunday discussion group, published a national newsletter, and is planning a video.[13] No one expected this from him. I suspect he amazed himself. He poured loving attention and his energy into a controversial project because that's what fully engrossed him. He believed in what he's doing. In return, his venture rewarded him with continuing vitality and—here and there—a bit of money.

Assess yourself to see if you've gained the three advantages of an authentic focus:

- How fully do I *immerse myself in what's truly desirable?* (How much time and energy do I waste daily worrying about obstacles or problems?)

- On a scale of 1 to 10, how effectively do I *manage my energy?*

- How successfully have I developed my ability to *manage my attention?*

Even if you direct your attention toward projects that matter, even if you learn to *manage* your energy and emotions, even if you grow into full, vibrant wholeness, no one can predict how life will turn out. The authentic person is always a mystery, enigmatically widening our vision of what's possible through a subtle, unpredictable unfolding.

## A SUMMARY STRATEGY

Three caterpillars responded differently to a butterfly that happened by: The first said, "Just look at that fellow, giving himself airs!" The second said, "How I'd love to fly like that!" The third said, "Why, that's me!"[14]

You'll discover what you love (or want) by attending to your intrinsic truths, your fulfillments, the *pattern* of your inherent delights.

*Try This:*
With respect to your working life, name ten "defining moments" when you felt, *"I was born to be or do this,"* and when money, approval, or status seemed irrelevant compared to the joy you got from your engagement with the task.

To begin restoring your authentic focus, ask yourself:

- To what do I attend when conflict, uncertainty or disappointment abound?
- To what have I *been* paying attention? (How helpful has that been?)
- What lifelong interests continue to fascinate me? Who— or what sort of person—earns a livelihood in those areas? What are they like?
- What tasks or jobs naturally call forth my most enjoyable, productive, concentrative abilities?
- What does the phrase "self-conditioning" mean to me within the context of my present working life and foreseeable future?
- If money—i.e., earning a living—weren't an object, how would I consciously choose to live? What would I *love* attending to?
- What three small *acts could I take today* (this week, next week, this month) to prepare for the life—or the work— I'd like?
- Locally—right here in my own community—whose business might I visit to get a realistic feel for the type of work I hope to create?
- What might be my remedies if, as mentioned in this chapter, the life I want to build (or the work I'd love to create) doesn't happen quickly, takes ten or more years to actualize? What support systems or back-up plan might I find to sustain my focus, manage frustration, shore up passion and hope?

# CHAPTER 3

# Meaningful Purpose

> *Frequently, your most intelligent strategy for*
> *creating work comes as you remain right where you*
> *are, save money, learn what more your aspirations*
> *require of you. If you have that luxury, this*
> *approach can smooth your ride to wherever it is*
> *you're headed.*

C onstancy of purpose, as Disraeli said, is the secret of success, particularly if you're striving to move beyond a traditional job-seeker's mentality. Meaningful purpose fans our wholesome desires, and that's motivating. Years ago (when I first contemplated leaving the public sector), a friend asked me, *"What exactly do you want out of life?"* Answering his seemingly innocuous question took years. But that helped me find my way and intensified my willingness to press forth.

You can inch—rather than race—toward a new career while responsibly meeting current obligations. This too is entrepreneurial—a disciplined strategy of mind and heart arising from your selective perspective designed to further personally meaningful aims. Staying put for the present minimizes obstacles and the potentially overwhelming nature of your transition.

No one can tell you what your purposes are. If you don't yet know how to convert your passions into a meaningful vocation, if you—like thousands of others—have never considered the topic seriously, then stay put and prepare for the long haul.

# Prepare for the Long Haul: Mara's Story

Frequently your most intelligent strategy for creating work comes by remaining right where you are, saving money, and learning what your aspirations require of you. If you have that luxury, this approach can smooth your ride to wherever it is you're heading.

Consider a woman I'll call Mara—a single mother who works full-time as a senior manager in a progressive, rapidly expanding corporation. Using the chart on page 15, I'd guess Mara to be a self-actualizing adult who increasingly views work as service or a gift of self. She's in the process of gradually reinventing herself—conceptualizing her life's vocation, chipping away at various financial limits or hesitations while also planning her next professional incarnation. Mara admits she is *consciously* readying herself for her future. She feels fortunate to be employed by a company that regularly advances her in responsibility. Mara sees a clear road to her objectives:

> My current position lets me uncover different tools that I'll need to study and gather ideas. *I'm not really ready to move on. I still feel a lot of fear. Of course I also have on-going obligations in raising my daughter alone.*

Mara wants her own counseling practice one day, "working with fairly healthy people who are on a spiritual path." It's apparently her vocation to help others stick with what's of value and encourage them:

> That's a highly intimate process, and I'm using my relationship with my daughter, as well as all my corporate ones, to learn what this entails. I'm not going to be a psychotherapist or a minister, but I'll use all of these skills in some eclectic mix.

I endure by reconceptualizing my relationship with my daughter as a practice in intimacy. Since I don't have a life-partner right now, parenting affords me some of the same challenges (of course not all) that marriage might. Seeing my role in this light takes the drudgery out of waiting for my goals to unfold and turns parenting into my personal development or spiritual work.

Notice how Mara's positive expectancy reframes her circumstances and lifts her day-to-day thinking. This alone adds to self-mastery. Mara says, "I'm growing personally and professionally through my corporate responsibilities. I'm using all these experiences to deepen and broaden myself."

A corporate job isn't always undesirable. You may be a waitress or a mechanic who longs to become part of a Fortune 500 work team. You know you'll need to earn a college degree, polish up your professional image, or refine some other element of your performance. This too is entrepreneurial in my view. This too calls for a long-range view.

The longer view is also shrewd. Cumulatively, you lose nothing: No relationship, no position, no mistake is for naught. You assimilate all experiences and fluctuating circumstances into your next step as you go. Creating work then becomes a buoyant, dynamic work-in-progress—one that enhances your entrepreneurial attitudes, no matter where you work. This is also how, to paraphrase Lord Chesterfield, we make life's pleasures our own—and therefore actually *taste* them.

Actress Whoopie Goldberg's story is an inspiring example of how long-term, meaningful purposes help to overcome potentially spirit-crushing struggles. By age eighteen, Goldberg was divorced and already the mother of a baby daughter. Because of harsh early circumstances, Goldberg reached her acting goals only by what might seem the lengthiest of paths. She *knew* she had acting talent and persisted despite continuous cruel rejections by the industry. Interviewing her on *60 Minutes,* journalist Ed Bradley said, "Even as her career began to move forward, Whoopie realized that talent wouldn't be enough."[1] Goldberg described some early trials:

> Going in and auditioning and having somebody say, "No, you can't play Eleanor of Aquitaine," I said, "Why not?" "You're black." I said, "So what?" They said, "Oh, but she was white." I said, "But this is the theater, honey. You know . . . this is make-believe. This is not real." It was like—they floored me.
>
> And of course getting into the movies, you know, was also like, "No, here—you can't do this; this girl's supposed to be from the Midwest." Like there were no black people in the Midwest, you know. So I get my feelings hurt a lot because I think . . . that I can do anything. It never occurs to me that there are things I can't do.[2]

Rushing impetuously toward ill-defined goals may also be passé. Moving slowly, you gain balance, poise, and self-understanding. Perhaps in your case, as in Goldberg's, talent isn't enough. You'll need to find ways around specific obstacles. Time helps you. "Waiting" lets you practice the art of nonresistance, to accept the inevitable with grace—without inordinate bitterness or frustration. This is a spiritual stance. Moreover, gradual change is usually more fruitful in the long run than is forced, ultra-aggressive upheaval. Undertaken wisely, steady transitions cultivate authenticity, groundedness, and virtues—like patience, compassion (for self and others), and perseverance. All these qualities improve your probability of success when, ultimately, you do figure out *how* to actualize your personal vision.

On the other hand, you may be fiercely impatient to move on—whether or not you're emotionally or financially ready. At forty-nine, a financial analyst told me she was burned out, eager for a career change, yet also frightened:

> My dream is to be a writer, yet I've always made "career security" my god. I'd bail out now, but some inner force grips me.

What say you: Is it possible to earn a living as an artist type? I'm scared, but yearning.

So goes much of my mail these days. I suspect that for every individual who asks for help by letter, or who visits career counselors, thousands more worry silently along precisely the same lines. Millions feel threatened by lurking, dark unknowns. Within this question's framework, let's explore some conservative ground rules for this sort of transition since an artist lives within each of us.

## Be Practical: Grow in "Down" Times

Repeatedly I'm asked, "In a dreary economic climate, can one still do work that one loves? Sometimes it's hard enough just to hold down a job." Repeatedly I answer, yes. Troubled times ask us to seriously rethink work; to plan for economic surprises; to envision both short- and long-term career adjustments; and to seek viable, fulfilling, vocational alternatives. And, no, not everyone is *ready* to create their livelihood.[3] I've already suggested that entrepreneurship depends on high-level inner stability and a deepened, ingenious consciousness. Centeredness—sound, steady emotional footing—is a requisite for people who want to create their work.

Creating work asks for (and develops) strict self-discipline and *discernment*—our ability to know what to do without being told. One sign that we lack the attributes of readiness is when we are conflicted. One man described how this feels:

I'm excited about the prospect of doing something radically different from my present work—opening a business with some pals or joining another good friend (in another state) as a helping professional. I have credentials but not money.

There's a part of me that feels stuck. Perhaps just lack

commitment for my current work; I'm excited—and scared as hell—about the downside risks to all of this. How does one assess honestly and accurately whether a situation is for one's highest good?

Indeed. How can one *know*? Our growth into an invigorating vocational life brings ever greater wisdom, right timing, our ability to "assess accurately" what to do. As we become full persons, our knack for "right action" and good judgment blossoms. Our decisions are, after all, existential ones. These happen within the context of our life and psyches. (A later chapter explores effective risk-taking and strategic planning in greater detail.) In the final analysis no one can tell us when to stay or to leave, or precisely when and how to exercise our courage. The question my friend posed long ago *("What do you really want out of life?")* seems worth asking periodically.

Does your present work let you grow in new directions? Does it exacerbate your fears or help you focus and widen your options? Which of these elements do you want in your life? Might you practice an aspect of the new thing (risky as it is) in a way that gives you necessary data as to its viability *before* you quit your secure job? I so love the Spanish proverb "God says, *'Choose what you will and pay for it,'*" which stresses that life holds no easy answers, that conscious choices are often costly ones. We must live with and pay for their consequences. Understanding this, we learn what it means to be fully human. Furthermore, we can exploit every delay as a cycle of growth. In our hurry-up culture, few of us have the disposition to use time as a resource, yet an authentic vocation unfolds our best life over *years;* it evolves as we yield to our truths.

Sometimes crisis or illness establishes a lengthy holding pattern. If we're forced to rest and restore ourselves, self-renewal makes our postponements more palatable. Setbacks may be blessings in disguise. Here is where we finally admit what's what, and acknowledge our doubts or brokenness. Most people tell me that their darkest times seeded their most significant growth. Crisis forces us to grapple with the real-world in a way that, as Thoreau said, "yields the most sugar . . . It is life near the bone where it is sweetest."[4]

A friend I'll call Hank lost his highly paid management job as a result of a merger. He grew seriously depressed. At first, he simply grieved. Then he vegetated. Then he admitted certain shadowy aspects of himself into view. Hank let himself see his own false ideas, felt how unhealthy choices had victimized him. This insight caused him further despair. He sustained feelings of intense loss and disappointment. Twice he spoke to me of suicide. Somehow, Hank eventually interpreted all his secret demons as allies. He talked with a counselor. He walked away from some old friends and drew closer to those companions offering real acceptance of who he is. He read deeply philosophical books and listened to self-help tapes. Hank's outer husks of choice revealed "corrective" inner work was in progress. Finally (*very* slowly, I should add), he bore forth a substantive optimism. Over a three-year period, a rich personal transformation took place.

Progressively, Hank found revitalizing interests and explored new lines of work. These blended his long-standing fascinations: finance, sales, love of the outdoors. Slowly, he forgave himself for whatever sins his guilt-phantoms accused him. Hank was healing. Energy and good humor returned, replacing lethargy and biting, hurtful sarcasm. Hank's self-styled *re-creation*, his investment of time and truth-telling mysteriously shaped good from that which had been "bad." This is decidedly inventive—entrepreneurial—and an aspect of how some people find meaningful purpose.

If we feel we have lost vision, energy, courage, faith, or our "fight" to live robustly and inventively, then—again, *while we're still employed*—we should seek counseling. I restate this periodically because sometimes, although we're *impatient* to start anew, we aren't ready. We defeat ourselves mentally even before taking a single step forward. Our cynicism or feelings of despair are signals telling us to get help.

Lacking readiness (to know exactly what to do), we'll find

ourselves unable to maneuver shrewdly through the rapids of our present circumstances. We must first *prepare* ourselves to identify and love our life's truths. *Then* we can go about the business of creating our work. This is not a hard and fast rule, just a conservative one. It is this love, after all, that as Thomas à Kempis taught "maketh light every heavy thing and beareth evenly every uneven thing."

## Determine Your Readiness—and Enthusiasm

Father Anthony De Mello tells of a woman who complained to her guru that riches hadn't brought her happiness. Her guru replied, "You speak as if luxury and comfort were ingredients of happiness, whereas all you need to be really happy, my dear, is something to be enthusiastic about."[5]

We *earn* our badges of readiness by confronting our heartfelt purposes and then committing to the struggle of actualizing them. Chapter Two introduced the first side of this coin: Genuine interests illuminate meaningful goals. But often this invites the very obstacles we loathe and *don't* want. Love—e.g., our enthusiasm for a vocation—helps us endure. For instance, many who enter the fields of acting or sales are secretly (or unconsciously) terrified of rejection. Their long-term purposes might be linked to performing or gaining prestige. Both sales and acting are professions that ruthlessly reject novices and the experienced alike. To call our hidden strengths into play, we need to feel, *"I'll pay anything to do this work."* Burning desire to be or do something gives us staying power—a reason to get up every morning or to pick ourselves up and start in again after a disappointment.

If you and I were working together to help you determine whether you're ready to create your own work, I'd ask you several questions. To start, I'd want to discuss some of the qualities outlined in our first chapter—to assess your personal history of inventiveness. With our discussion about *authentic focus* in mind, I'd certainly notice if you have the maturity or "heart" to stay lovingly absorbed in your goals. I'd inquire about your work habits, your background, and keenest interests. I'd steer you away from thinking about your work as a *corporate function* (or as a specific salary grade or title) and would listen carefully as you described your most enjoyable tasks, to uncover what achievements come naturally, bring distinct pleasure, and what others say you're good at. I'd have you list the sorts of tasks you're doing when time seems to evaporate or pass quickly. I'd try to hear if you can articulate your long-term vision, whether you have the audacity to strive for excellence at something and whether you have a reasonable degree of enthusiasm for what you *love* to do—both now and in a few years' time.

All the while, I'd listen to your underlying attitudes about work, to determine whether your *purposes* mean anything to you in a deep, heartfelt way. I'd try to evaluate whether your work ethic, focus, judgment and *actual track record* are commensurate with the responsibilities you *say* you want.

Sometimes we feel so worn down by our spirit-breaking, daily grind (or a serious loss, like being fired) that we lack the energy and hope needed to reach our goals. The creative process makes demands on us. In and of itself, it can trigger anxiety, conflict, chronic fatigue, and even intense *resistance* (what I've called the Big R)—the recoil, or withdrawal of energy from obligations. When apathy or restlessness undercut our plans, the Big R is usually lurking close by.[6]

One person expressed anger at the realities her ambition brought. She wanted to quit her detested nine-to-five job *immediately*. But her desired work wouldn't instantly support her and her family:

> I'm tired and cynical and all those other things you mention that point to our unhappiness with a job. I hate Mondays because I don't know how I can make it through another week

without going stark, raving mad. I'm getting on in years and want to make my move. I'm bored and tired. Is there any help for me? I can't afford therapy, so don't even suggest it.

The bare truth is I *can't* prescribe a quick, comforting, or scripted answer for anyone, least of all someone who feels this way. If you're tired, cynical, and feel like "going stark, raving mad," you *do* need therapy and also a thorough physical check-up, even if you don't want me to say so.

An associate said, "Almost everyone who experiences themselves out of work or transitioning into new work feels some sort of 'low-grade' depression. What's the difference between suffering from not being in the right vocation and serious depression?"

Clinical depression is more than situational suffering (although this too may call for short-term counseling). It is an inner adversary affecting an estimated 17 million Americans. It masquerades as lethargy, disinterest, procrastination, and low enthusiasm. Ask anyone who's suffered from a bout of it: "*Feeling* depressed is one of two major symptoms. The other is . . . markedly diminished interest in food, sex, hobbies—just about everything pleasurable."[7] Joylessness bankrupts us. A physician's input (not just a psychologist's) is warranted if you're plagued by boredom, fatigue, pessimism, or bottled-up, impotent rage. There are other symptoms, too many to list here. If you're not sure what ails you, check with a competent professional.* How could you—how could anyone—experiencing feelings of despair attend positively to the pressing tasks of creating (or unfolding) a vocation, one *element* of which could well be starting up a business of some sort? Your deepest purpose involves awakening to who *you* are—as a particular person. Your sadness (or fear and rage) may be testimony to your not having fulfilled the tasks of *your* vocation.

---

*For more information on depression, you may wish to contact the National Mental Health Association (800-969-6642) or your family doctor.

Short of miracles, therapy of some sort could be needed to help you launch your entrepreneurial ship. Creating a profitable, enjoyable vocation depends on passion, intrinsic motivation, and an enduring beneficent vision. If you're a healthy skeptic, that's one thing. If you're cynical, resentful, or depressed, get help.

As explained more fully in Chapter Seven, experienced entrepreneurs are actually *artists* at heart. They use all the means at their disposal, including the entirety of their inner life—moods, laziness, "wildness," their delicate incongruities—to serve their dreams. They also take their "down times" seriously, in part because negativity is costly; it saps creative drive.

Bear in mind readiness can come at any age. You probably have many more years to work and can do much more with yourself than you now imagine. I remember one woman of eighty-something (just gearing up an at-home editing business) who was enviably excited about her future. Another case in point: When a young minister asked an elderly preacher (in his eighties) what his secret was for high energy and superior productivity, the older man answered: "I am intensely interested in what I'm doing." Expressing your enthusiasms can add years of creative life to your time on earth.

# Make Honest Self-Assessments

Some people seem incapable of seeking *any* long-term goal. Emotionally immature, they're ill-suited to examine their lives deeply, to postpone gratification, or persist with steady follow-through. They grow hopeless in the face of discouraging feedback. They crave reassurance or comfort, and cling to the security of the familiar, no matter what the cost. "Big dreams" that ask them to move forward seem foreboding. But the price of living a safe, constricted existence is also dearly expensive. Persistent stress, low self-regard, and joylessness are some costs.

Balance seems in order here. When you proceed, as did Whoopie Goldberg, with faith and simple childlike trust (neither impulsively rushing forward nor hesitating inordinately), then you "emulate water." As the I Ching oracle puts it:

When flowing water . . . meets with obstacles on its path, a blockage in its journey, it pauses. It increases in volume and strength, filling up in front of the obstacle and eventually spilling past it. . . .

Do not turn and run, for there is nowhere worthwhile for you to go. Do not attempt to push ahead into the danger . . . emulate the example of the water: Pause and build up your strength until the obstacle no longer represents a blockage.[8]

It is human to be fearful, impulsive, or resistive. These words describe most of us at some point in life. Before starting a new business or changing jobs, assess yourself honestly. Where you find weakness, commit to repairing yourself on the inside. That's a first step and one way to increase skill and strength. Eventually all apparent obstacles give way, if only because you've had that shift of mind which lifts you beyond obstacles. That's an awakening—a spiritual impetus—with practical, entrepreneurial consequences.

No one is perfect. Acknowledging our imperfections, we are forewarned of problems. Hesitation, depression or envy of those who *appear* to have what we want are often signs of weakness or lack of vigorous, clear purpose. These feelings may be saying we're not yet ready to *create* our good. When we're emotionally *un*prepared, we want something for nothing, and quickly.

*Smart Money*, a *Wall Street Journal* publication, describes this tendency through the story of one couple who meet, fall in love (on an amorous South Seas holiday), and marry after a two-week, whirlwind courtship. They don't know each other, and they've given zero thought to the business venture about which they fantasize. Finally, they're reported to have made a poor investment—

with only superficial planning and without preparedness. Titled "Tale from Dropout Hell," the piece illustrates now *not* to approach right livelihood—or anything else for that matter:

> As they swooned through a vacation in the Caribbean at a romantic hotel that was for sale, the idea washed over them: Let's chuck everything and go run a little inn. In the end though, the lovely inn they bought, with its fireplaces and antiques and rustic flavor, not only ate up all of their money. It also ate up their marriage.[9]

Consider on the other hand, Mara—the single parent mentioned earlier—who meets her current responsibilities while readying herself for the future. Mara has allowed herself a period of seasoning. She's rounding herself out (as a person) and keeping her genuine purposes ever in mind, even as she fulfills her present duties. There are countless individuals like Mara who *invest* their talents quietly, patiently. They bide their time until retirement or their last child graduates from college and seem to embody Epictetus' soothing counsel: Learn to wish that everything comes to pass exactly as it does. This too is spiritual.

To the impulsive couple, reality involved no patience, no lengthy seasoning. It meant "endless work, demanding guests, stress, and money pressures."[10] They sought easy, pain-free work and romance. Perhaps they imagined their existence would be like a television fantasy. Alas, reality annihilates anyone who thinks this way.

# No Guarantees; No "Something for Nothing"

Fritz Perls, the founder of the Gestalt school of therapy, suggests that in the extreme, resistance and confusion involve the "dummy complex"—a stupefying neurosis, traceable to unrealistic notions developed in infancy, during nursing.

Suppose an infant clings to its mother's breast (or to its bottle) *long* after all the milk is gone. Imagine that baby won't let go of the nipple, grows sleepy, or bored. It exerts no effort but expects food to come without exercising its sucking muscles. If baby never figures out that hanging on to thumb, pacifier, or empty bottle doesn't produce a flow of milk, then baby easily can become someone who expects something for nothing. Such seems the lot of too many adults (dare I suggest too many *Americans?*).

> From this nursing profile we learn that a child should be brought up on the lines of . . . the "reality principle," the principle which says "yes" to the gratification but demands that the child be able to endure the suspense of [effort]. It should be prepared to do some work in exchange for [what it wants] . . .[11]

You may wonder how an infant's feeding habits could possibly affect adult vocation. Early impressions and patterns color our later worldview—and our productivity. Adults frequently have inappropriate, unrealistic work habits. We Americans are famous for craving easy, instant, ever-flowing food (mental or material). This is not all bad; our country was founded by those who wanted to build a better mousetrap. However, when bright, physically healthy, attractive individuals want *everything* precisely as, and when, they want it—instantly and effortlessly—a whole nation's quality of concentration, service, and products suffers. The wish for instant gratification undermines the strengths of *both* individual and collective enterprise.

Inheriting money to start a business (or earning scads of it quickly) is no assurance of lasting success. The quick-money-fix may even handicap you. You could believe you've "made it" and grow sloppy, partake in excesses, lose all your savings. Without true financial acumen—which generally comes with time and hands-on experience—it's so easy to squander cash reserves.

Moreover, enhanced *levels* of insight and understanding arrive with each advance in our consciousness of enterprise. Time and experience are teammates that help us shape a meaningful life. Be forewarned: Entrepreneuring is an endeavor for grown-ups, who have skills, patience, and discernment. Those with fast-food time frames or "magical thinking" mentalities should seek elsewhere for answers.

## Tackle Your True Work

Identifying your enthusiasms requires courage and heroic creative vision. You have to believe that what you want is possible *for you*. It takes audacity to consider new realities—to simplify life by paring down to bare essentials, to accept a lesser salary or forgo fringe benefits—or to reach for fulfillment when you watch your parents or friends living far below their potentials.

Most people who have relinquished a job (or been fired or retired from one) grieve and feel lost for a time. At such times, without positive role models and stories to support imagination, our thoughts can be perilous. Stories, mythic heroes, and even motion-picture characters help us build possibility tracks for our new objectives. By these we travel into revised, more desirable realities. By this I mean it's possible to mentally construct images of what we want and use these as rough sketches for the behaviors and attitudes we need.

For example, if you told me that you felt a gnawing sense that you're missing your life, but can't figure out what your passions are, I might ask you to watch a movie or two where the heroes, though temporarily bewildered about their lives, circuitously locate life's purposes. *Regarding Henry* or *Defending Your Life* are superb teachers. The simplest movie is, potentially, an emotional eye-opener that is rich with sensory data, archetypal myths, and universal conflicts. We can see, and revise, ourselves in almost all decent stories.[12]

Some people just decide, "This is what I'll do. This is what I want." They may not *feel* called in the classic, subjective way. No inner voice or beams of light summon them. They simply choose—consciously—what they want, without all the hocus-pocus of meditation, visualization, or inward listening. However, many others get stuck somewhere along this choice route, in part because they believe they "can't" have a desirable life, or perhaps because choosing one thing means giving up another. They want to walk down all roads simultaneously, and this impedes progress. So they wait and wait. Responsible choice involves consequences, not the least of which are relinquishments all along our way.*

Myths, fairy tales, and fables (like those in movies) offer timeless messages from the collective unconscious and can spark fresh insight. If you're moved by a story's outcome or by what happens to a character, if you befriend (instead of shut down) your feelings, you can "see" *your* meanings, feel who you are at best, or worst, and even find ways to invent new scripts about who you want to be.[13]

## Enthusiasms Reveal Purposes

You can begin to create your work by staying your course, by sticking with things you don't particularly like, and by practicing a mental discipline of focusing on, and actively preparing for, what you want.

Even in situations not particularly suited to us, we can develop new abilities: A shy person can gain social ease by selling cars, vacuum cleaners, or Tupperware. An extrovert can learn to like

---

*If you don't feel you've *found* life's deeper meanings yet, then consider reading Richerd N. Bolles's *How to Find Your Mission in Life* (Ten Speed Press). It's short, sweet, and simply put and clarifies what could be a daunting philosophical inquiry. Bolles views work in its largest, most generous context and his writings seem a perfect study-companion to this chapter. If you prefer a Zen Buddhist framework, see Laurence G. Boldt's *Zen and the Art of Making a Living* (Penguin), a rich, informative text.

working in solitary, focused settings. A technical specialist can become a good manager of people. People *do* grow by enduring what isn't pleasant, by building tough resolve and perseverance in the process.[14] Such choices teach us gradually to endure, expand self-awareness or become familiar with the costs and consequences of our acts. All work done mindfully rounds us out, helps complete us, as persons.

Still, the reality is that people's motives and temperaments differ. Scripture warns that some of us, despite our varied talents, dig about in the earth and *bury* our gifts and our genuine intentions. Then the cosmos somehow reckons with us, if only by extinguishing our potentials and our joy.[15]

If you're not able (or willing) to assume the tough task of finding a meaningful purpose, if you're unenthusiastic or resentful about most things, if you can't (or won't) cultivate two careers simultaneously, or if you recoil from honest self-scrutiny as you prepare for your future, then you'd best rethink your vocational dreams and get cozy with the job-classified ads.

In truth, you're *never* out of work. No matter how things look, you always have a job, and it is spiritual in the main. The significant business of your life is alive and well, awaiting discovery, within your very soul. You and I were born to come into ourselves as complete and distinctive persons. Accepting this, we build a valuable life. This is the hidden, undergirding occupation beneath anyone's meaningful purpose. Pushcart merchant, Wall Street banker, and Olympic athlete alike find "meaningful purposes" as they animate their essential authenticities through whatever vocational expressions define them uniquely.

We need high *spiritual intelligence* to comprehend this, as Chapter Seven elaborates, because our own unfolding asks us to discern what is, at first blush, *imperceptible*—an inner liveliness. It takes intuition and not a little grace to "hold" such slippery truths, to *grasp* our purpose, to understand what now is unknown or unseen. Feelings, aspirations, and bits of interior stuff ultimately form our emerging self. Refining ourselves as *specific* persons, making outer world conditions conform to our subjective verities is hard, illusive work. Who, having such a luscious assignment, could ever be "unemployed"?

## A SUMMARY STRATEGY

Once upon a time, there lived a very intelligent woman who *felt* her destiny vividly but couldn't quite verbalize it. One day, a friend took her to see the film *Enchanted April.* Watching, she knew she'd finally found her purpose:

*The lush scenery and natural beauty of those flower gardens, the melting of the characters' hearts was immensely significant to me. I saw the film again and again, immersing myself in its moods. Suddenly I realized that my own heart yearned for love, for beauty, for compassion. That (not some special job, house, or location) is what I seek. I'll give my all to be in that profoundly spiritual state.* That's *my purpose.*

*Try This:*

- Start an "Inspirational Scrapbook." Keep track of whatever uplifts, inspires, and encourages you. Find stories, photographic images, lines of poetry, or works of art that speak to you *nonverbally.* Give yourself the gift of time to simmer your impressions and listen to your inner voice. Curb your impatience to know *immediately* and explicitly what your life's purpose is.
- What stories inspire you (or show how you've thwarted yourself)? What characters uplift you or point out goals you feel are worth pursuing? Reflect on the *pattern* of movies and books that you typically seek out. How do

these stories illuminate or rekindle your hope, your dormant life-affirming energies?

Without *over*thinking or censoring, quickly write down your answers:

- What kinds of tales restore me, so that—despite fatigue or negative feelings—my optimism and affirming drives are revived?
- What heroes or heroines do I routinely admire? What admirable or energizing characteristics do they project? How might my attraction to them add to my self-knowledge, reveal what I need, value, or want?
- What movies would I want shown, studied and discussed in, say, my child's class or in a prison, an elder-care, or veteran's rehabilitation center? Why?
- What movies (stories) remind me of how my life could be at its best?

Now review all your answers. If possible, add to and embellish your list. Briefly complete these sentences:

- If my *current* life were a movie, to what extent would I be interested in it?
- What plot (or script) changes would I need to make to respect myself as a substantive character, or to enrich and make meaningful my own performance?
- How might I revise my life's script in order to enjoy and fully "encounter" my own life?
- The heroes/heroines I admire most inspire me because . . .

# CHAPTER 4

# "Figuring-out" Skills

*Your vocation and the answers related to it belong
to you, are meant for you—like a perfect love or
soul mate. Yet often we play a kind of adult
hide-and-seek before finding (or inventing) our
vocation.*

An entrepreneur's creative process is often a luxurious, sensual experience. We overlook the *pleasures* we might receive from work at great peril to both heart and pocketbook. Creative people experience dynamic *joy* by doing their favorite activities. Subjectively, they sense themselves growing stronger, distinctive, competent. In a vocational sense, when who we are fits what we do, we feel exuberant: A fiddler feels most powerful when fiddling and cobalt blue excites the artist's eye as fresh foie gras does the chef's. Abraham Maslow felt there was a "pre-established harmony" in this, that between work and worker one sensed a "good match like the perfect love affair or friendship . . . or a key and lock."

The adage, "What you don't use, you lose," also suggests our gifts and interests may atrophy if ignored. Exercised, these are strengthened. With the enhancement of, say, sales or research skill we gain competence. Now, instead of submitting to the world's demands, we begin to have what it takes to ask the world to adapt to us. Furthermore, each obstacle we successfully surmount adds to such expertise. Our next initiatives then summon up yet greater finesse for ever-greater independence and self-sufficiency. This phenomenon has less to do with being a maverick than with having vision, that is, a clear idea of what we want and how—in our area of mastery—things should be done. Figuring-out skills seem an inherent ingredient in possessing such authority as our next story illustrates.

# Shanalei's Story

When Shanalei decided to move from Hawaii to Northern California, she knew the change in location would necessitate a change in careers. Shanalei needed meaningful work and wanted to use her talents to serve others. Lacking formal education, she assessed her previous experiences (as well as her interests and passions) to figure out how to create her optimal future:

> I'm highly motivated and want to do my best, so I'm always learning from whatever I'm doing. Being in small business in general taught me a lot. I asked myself, "What can I do?" I don't have a college education, so I don't have specific training. I knew the real estate and travel-industry business, and that was about it. Then I realized I also knew the gift-basket business. That was the "light bulb" I needed.

Shanalei derives her figuring-out skill, in part, from an entrepreneur's perspective that says what she wants is possible for her to acquire, through her own creativity. She didn't know it at the time, but all her previous endeavors had helped her build self-confidence and viable business skills:

> In my real estate business and as a director of operations for an events planning firm I'd gained practical business experience. I knew how to budget. I was good at allocating sums of money

to this or that activity. I negotiated with independent contractors and came within our targeted profit margin. In other words, I had a track record. My skills and talents made profits for others. But I didn't see the point in just continuing to put money in the pocket of people who already had it. I wanted independence, a chance to serve others, and work that added real meaning to my life.

In Shanalei we find that key and lock—the good fit that Maslow described. I suspect love for some high purpose, even enjoyment—certainly not mad ambition—drove Shanalei to establish her own company. As her comments reveal, Shanalei loves people and thrives on expressing her values of beauty and service.

To be successful in my business, you truly have to like people, not just pretend to. I wanted to do something for others. And I observe people constantly helping me too. My work gives me a real high; my intentions are good and good things keep returning to me.

Enjoyment, the love of challenge and self-mastery (not workaholism) lets entrepreneurs see and experiment in ways that are out of the ordinary. Workaholics churn out largely unnecessary, often useless activity. Their whirl of busy-ness is empty, generally devoid of pleasure, and designed to stave off fear, rage, or frustration. The distractions of an overcrowded schedule protect workaholics from having to relax or relate intimately.

This is *not* what motivates those positively engaged with their authentic vocation. Then *love* drives labor. Beware: These two work profiles often *appear* the same. Yet when love fuels you, your thoughts and acts are more an intuitive dance than a stressed-out, robotic march. Pleasure enables Shanalei to fulfill her goals:

Anyone who doesn't love their work isn't going to hang in there during the down times. I didn't start my business just to make money. People always say to me, "Oh creating food and wine baskets seems like so much fun!" but they don't see the dogwork, the detail, the marketing. I wear many hats. In the beginning it was only me. I had to be certain I was comfortable with the things I didn't like doing.

It is our collective shame that educational, governmental, and traditional corporate organizations so grossly misunderstand this issue. In fact, our institutions are frequently prejudiced against improvisers and the energetically inventive. Creativity expert E. Paul Torrance, a foremost researcher of giftedness, insists that the creative among us routinely face discrimination:

> Many people misinterpret the motivations of highly creative individuals who can't seem to stop working. Few creative individuals can stand the pressure of working only a forty-hour week. This is *interpreted** as an attempt to outdo others, rise to a position of power or favor or such. Creative individuals, however, do not usually care for power and some of the other usual rewards. The exercise of their creative powers is itself a reward, and to them, the most important reward. . . . *The creative individual is unable to stop working because he can't stop thinking. To him, there is nothing more enjoyable than work in which he can use his creative powers.**[1]

As you consider your figuring-out skills, remember that genuine interests and meaningful goals are linked. Without *first* identifying these two, you may miss the sheer *fun* of engaging with your dynamic concerns. Your vocation and the answers related to it belong to you, are *meant* for you—like a perfect love or soul mate. Yet, often, we must undergo a kind of adult hide-and-seek before finding (or inventing) our vocation.

---

*Author's italics for emphasis.

# "Messing Around" for Answers

Entrepreneurs find their answers circuitously. They may pursue a fascination for years, or weave back and forth between intense frustrations and their desire to hit the mark of some inner ideal. Their hunt for answers eventually unfolds uniqueness. Entrepreneurs are also resourceful. They find answers by a "random messing around without following an explicit plan."[2] Whether you hope to create a part-time or home business or simply wish to fathom the true nature of your vocation, Shanalei's seemingly haphazard methods of sleuthing may guide your steps:

> I play with answers and rarely concentrate on negatives. I've seen friends get caught up in their problems—overwhelmed by fear. I've had that happen too briefly. But that's dangerous. I prefer to constantly look at what I can do, write down everything I can imagine to solve a problem. I scan my lists, notice possibilities. Near my desk I keep Eleanor Roosevelt's saying, "The future belongs to those who believe in their dreams."
>
> I also keep pictures handy that let my mind soar and change these frequently. It's helpful to surround myself with things that make me feel good—you know, things that are pleasing to the eye.
>
> In my old job, I surrounded my computer with pictures of my goal—postcards of my destination (in Northern California). Those reminded me why I was slaving away at two jobs, scrimping and saving to start my own company.

If there are two kinds of people in the world—those who seek explicit how-to directions for doing everything and those who chuck instructions and figure things out alone—then entrepreneurs fall into the latter category. Preoccupied with relevant problems, most entrepreneurs enjoy probing the unknown, *like*

89

messing around for answers.[3, 4] Frequently, this "play" makes entrepreneurs seem inaccessible.

Creative adults frequently complain of being lonely, of being unable to talk to their peers. They may feel isolated. This could deepen over time, become severe with age, widened responsibility, or notable achievement. Nor should we assume that involvement with one's own delights and projects generates instant answers—or popularity. Even our friends can reject us if we are too "different."[5] Our renegade's nature, our love of what we're doing, and above all, our tendency to follow our heart's call, make us unpredictable companions. Corporate supervisors, classroom teachers, and parents all know how difficult managing self-actualizing, creative people can be.

When he was a boy, Gary Blew ordered a direct-mail taxidermy course. He quickly discarded all instructions after briefly scanning them. Blew explains, "There was too much artist in me, even then, to follow the recommended procedures." According to *Washington* magazine, Blew is "now regarded . . . as one of the best [taxidermists] in his business. It's the execution that sets Blew apart."[6] It pays to invest in one's inherent wisdoms when solving problems, and entrepreneurial types tend to strike out on their own: They, like Blew, prefer their own to other people's directions. When such individuals find their niche, they will spend hours each day engrossed in their pursuits. Like other self-starters, Blew says, "What I do pleases me, and isn't that what it's all about?"[7]

## Uniqueness Holds Answers

*Entrepreneurs improve our collective wisdom.* Margaret Mead, the brilliant anthropologist, was a world-class original. Robert Schwartz of the Tarrytown Conference Center once said that Mead elevated common sense to a new level. I've also heard Mother Teresa described in much this way: as a shrewd strategist and gifted negotiator who transcends political boundaries to bring a healing touch to the dying or raise funds to serve the needy around the globe. She has been called the world's most powerful woman. This is said not to diminish Mother Teresa's spirituality. Yet, neither must we discount her nearly supernatural entrepreneurial skill. Like all superb improvisers, her accomplishments make one wonder, "How does she do it?" or "Why didn't *I* think of that?"

The news recently reported the story of a man who had lost everything: his job, his home, his family. He may have been living in his car when *it* was stolen by a car-jacker during a wave of urban car-jackings. The car theft was his last straw. Enraged, he became determined to foil future assaults.

With a meager assortment of tools and materials, he invented a computerized car-protection device. Installed, it allows its car's rightful owner to step into a phone booth, dial an 800 number, and immobilize the stolen car so that it can be retrieved. I hear that homeless inventor is now patenting his invention (and that he's no longer without means). This man's ingenuity elevates our collective wisdom, illustrates what *we* might do. Entrepreneurs fulfill their aims while helping us fulfill ours.

*Entrepreneurs trust the mystery of the unknown.* Rather than accepting imprisonment by what they don't understand, entrepreneurs strive to transcend their questions and limits. Often this means trusting idiosyncrasies, going against convention, and devising belief systems that say trying something new is *possible.*

This is not to suggest that entrepreneurs don't experience self-doubts or that mental fog that precedes most tough choices. When we are heavily invested in a matter, it's human to lie awake nights wondering what course of action is best. This is when it's productive to talk to a trusted friend or counselor and listen to ourselves describe our apprehensions. This too is when it helps to know how we solve problems most effectively.

*Entrepreneurs study their own discovery process.* Some perfect it as an art in itself, and delight in solving problems through their own ways of figuring out. Perhaps awe or wonder led Shanalei into her current business. After all, as she admitted earlier, she loves people, creating beautiful gifts, and serving others. Now, however, the problems arising from her consciously chosen work help her develop her self, not just her enterprise. The longer Shanalei and entrepreneurs like her persist, the more they learn what it means for *them* to be uniquely human. Comprehending this is a key element to building a fulfilling life. Successful entrepreneurs ultimately *trust* their own way of doing things. (This relates to our next chapter's discussion of risk taking and illustrates the synergy between all these inner attributes.) For example, Shanalei remembers having to make tough judgment calls in childhood:

> I was born to a very young, single mother. We moved around a lot. My mother worked around the clock to support us. She was very loving, but I also had to be responsible early in life. Then, in high school, I chose not to move with her—to stay on my own. I was ready for full independence. I didn't want to live by her decisions—I didn't like what I saw her doing. Now I constantly marvel at how easy life is—adulthood sure beats what I faced then.

Effective solution finders tend to face their tough issues quickly. When political media adviser Roger Ailes was retained by the Reagan campaign, he instinctively spotted sticky issues, "cut to the heart of the matter and asked Reagan: 'What are you going to do when they say you're too old for the job?' "[8] This razorlike question slices away confusion. Figuring out involves eliminating illusions.

That archetypal entrepreneur Malcolm Forbes felt problems were a natural by-product of being alive. Whether motorcycling, hot-air ballooning, or publishing his magazine, he got a "kick" out of life. Perhaps problems stimulated his mind:

> I don't think anybody can be a success who doesn't like what they do . . . [But it's] no job if it has no challenge; there's

nothing to it if there are no problems . . . but the essential thing is liking what you're doing.[9]

# Creative Adapters:
# Masters at Figuring Out

What I've previously called *creative adaptation* describes this mentality. Creative adapters don't simply adjust, they improvise answers with superior figuring-out skills, meeting a crisis or the unknown artfully, especially in their areas of interest.[10] One entrepreneur admitted, "It's *fun* not knowing what to do— learning for oneself how to get from A to B. If my job wasn't baffling at times, I wouldn't enjoy it."

Creative adapters invent their best futures, successfully bending conventions to accommodate their life's authentic purposes. Productive self-beliefs support their optimism and the experimentation needed to further their sense that, "I'll eventually figure out what to do, even if I don't know what that is yet." This is also the very idea that reinforces healthy self-esteem.

To move from the fantasy of an idealized job to creating economically remunerative work, it's not enough to be a renegade. You must demonstrate real-world skill. This entails modifying the unhelpful notions you now entertain about yourself.[11] Productive *self*-ideas contribute to both work fulfillment and security.

Parkhurst Quimby, the enlightened healer (and forefather of what is popularly called the New Thought Movement) taught that *what we believe, we create.*[12] He meant that our deepest beliefs steer actions, influence well-being, and generally determine our quality of life.

If you review Don's, Mara's, and Shanalei's commentaries, you'll find liberating self-ideas. Don says, "Without experience, I started my company." Mara tells us, "I'm inventing my life's vocation as I go." Shanalei remarks: "I play with answers. I notice possibilities and rarely concentrate on negatives." What do *your* conversations say about your self-beliefs? Do your words and self-descriptions enable your creative skills, let you sustain the tensions of change? Or, does your own everyday language discourage you, and cause you to run from unknowns?

## Productive Self-Notions

It has been said that heroes (or heroines) are people with courage enough to make something good out of their lives. This describes entrepreneurs as well. Their self-biases give them the drive to reach their objectives. Self-ideas are complex *systems* of belief. When productive, these idea networks give us inventive power, propel us beyond the restraints of convention. Self-beliefs color our attitudes, choices, "luck," and interpersonal relationships. A brief examination of these illustrates how each nurtures—or thwarts—our ability to create our work.

### *"I Have What It Takes to 'Get Real'"*

This self-bias lets us view ourselves as capable, or gradually outgrowing our limits and resistances. Our old view (of recoil from certain challenges) amounts to living in *un*reality, the past, how we wish things were. Perhaps we want someone to support us financially, while in actuality we must earn our own way. Or we wish our traditional corporate job would last forever even though we know it's being eliminated. Our self-bias, *"I have what's needed to 'get real,'"* motivates us to accept the inevitable, to step out beyond fear. We build this self-idea through action, not just through fancy words. By updating our resume or returning that dreaded phone call, we lessen self-doubt and strengthen our chances for developing financial security or self-reliance.

Most of us cling to lifeless, unproductive ideas (and even people). The man who believes he's all washed up at fifty and the woman who believes that because of her gender she can't break through the corporate glass ceiling are both slaves to their circumstances. Advanced age, economic obstacles, or educational limits are only insurmountable barriers to success when dark thoughts control the mind's picturing powers. Anyone who's ever needlessly worried about the future has felt the horror of such demons. In part, the optimism born of controlling fear comes from getting real—tangling with reality, learning not to quit.

There are gradations to "getting real." Our earliest victories, however meager, prepare us for our next hurdles. During Earl Graves's boyhood, getting real meant laboring around the clock to secure a stable financial future. When the well-known publisher was a high schooler in Brooklyn's Bedford-Stuyvesant area, he worked three jobs to survive and made it through college holding down several other jobs. By his junior year, while living in a dormitory, he created a landscaping business. After graduation he became a realtor and within three months sold nine houses.

In 1965, Graves began working for the Justice Department—a position that ultimately landed him a job with former New York Senator Robert Kennedy. Kennedy coached Graves into more rarified levels of "getting real." According to an article in *Black Enterprise,* the experience was valuable in part because, "Kennedy . . . was totally unfamiliar with failure, and insisted on success."[13] Once the senator asked Graves to contact then-Secretary of the Interior Morris Udall (who was rafting in Colorado). When Graves told Kennedy that he couldn't reach Udall, Kennedy replied, "Graves, that raft is not going down that river all day. It's going to stop somewhere and when it does I want Udall standing there with a phone in his hand!" Graves concludes, "You would be surprised how many people quit when faced with obstacles. As every good salesman knows, everything may not be possible today, but sooner or later, it is possible."[14]

Any athlete who's ever trained past an injury understands the irony of "getting real." To meet our own standard of success, we simultaneously must use whatever ingenuity or power we possess while refusing to fail. This means moving into, then beyond, weaknesses even as we accept our limits. We are willing to express our *strengths,* do battle with resistance, and somehow be empathetic with what we are at the same time. One man confided, "I had to teach myself I deserved success." Another said, "I'm learning not to be too reasonable!" Entrepreneurs use their daily obstructions to practice getting real.

## "I Create a Fit Between My Interests and the Needs of the Marketplace"

We all have talents that dovetail with the needs of others. Establishing a productive meshing of what we love to do and what others need is *art.* Here's an example of that: Once on a long plane trip, before taking a nap, I had an extended conversation with my seat partner. She was openly worried about her teenage son who had two loves: art and medicine. The boy wanted to become a doctor, but felt torn in equal parts between medical school and an illustrator's career. We discussed his conflict for a bit; then I took my nap. During that few minutes' rest, I dreamed the lad was a medical illustrator. Later I shared the dream with my new acquaintance, whereupon she instantly cheered up. She felt this was the perfect resolution, and said her son would love medical illustration.

This is the sort of lock and key we each must create. A scientist who loves art or music or photography can construct a lucrative synthesis of technical and artistic talents. There's nothing radical about such blends. However, heightened self-awareness raises the probability of our figuring out such answers. Dreams, hunches, flashes of clarity, synchronously helpful meetings with the right book or person are all allies of our elevated awareness.

Imagine, for example, what you'd do if you wanted to polish swords in this space age. Tatsuhiko Konno, the only samurai sword conditioner in the Pacific Northwest (and one of only three in America), shows how a creative synergy serves self and others. Konno became enchanted with swords during his boyhood in

Japan when he competed in *kendo* (or fencing). Gradually, he evolved his knowledgeable expertise in the martial arts, blade polishing, and sword restoration. Today Konno is a recognized master. In an impromptu teleconference, he told me not many people can do his sort of work:

> Very few Westerners are prepared for such discipline. In Japan we traditionally dedicate ourselves to one job for at least ten years. We study at least seven years under a master in our chosen field. Even now I continually increase my skills. I go back to Japan every year to study with the master sword polishers there. People like us are considered National Treasures—like top artists.

Konno admits his is not a very lucrative vocation. Although he has virtually no competition (in the United States there are an estimated 200,000 samurai sabers), Konno's craft requires enormous outlays of time and patience. One writer described Konno's workmanship this way:

> His task is to bring out the exquisite landscape of the temper line, the heart and strength of the weapon. His twelve-step polishing process can take up to ten days to complete, though the polishing may last thirty to fifty years on a well-maintained weapon.[15]

Like all gifted artists, Tatsuhiko Konno feels his work is "a sacred task. I love this work and the restoration of these old blades. Many are museum pieces. That's why I can do it—because I love it."

Similarly, whether we are parents, coaches, health care workers, city cab drivers, or medical illustrators, we can dovetail our needs with those of others. Our rendering of true service to others is our best insurance against economic downturns or competition, but this cannot be accomplished if we don't find ways to meet the needs of the marketplace.

## *"I'm an Active Solution-Finder"*

It's human to wish that things weren't as they are—to dream about an easy, perfect life or impressive, prestigious goals. Only the rare person methodically *acts* in ways that further his or her dreams, every day. The active solution finder employs all inner faculties (e.g., hunches or imagination) *and* the best external data to "sell" or market their abilities and ideas. These habits strengthen learning.

We may simply use pen and paper to record our daily goals or use the calendar to monitor our progress. We might reward ourselves for completing tough tasks, or in some other consistent way assess, then upgrade, our performance. We don't do this because someone is peering judgmentally over our shoulder, supervising every move, but because we love being competent. Our enjoyment carries none of the emotional baggage of the "I must/I should" injunction. We simply notice when we're *not* using time or attention fruitfully. Gently, we correct ourselves, elevating self-respect, our standards, and work habits in the process. Soon, high functioning *self-*management becomes our new objective—one shared with other assertive, responsible adults.

This is not to suggest that only aggressive forward movement is useful. High functioning adults continually address their needs for rest, renewal and change of pace. Active solution-finding depends on our devising schedules for such *active passivity*. In other words, we practice what Buddhists may call *non-doing*. Even if we meditate on a silent subterranean level, we can move forward. The healthiest entrepreneurs, artists, and gifted scientists routinely "do nothing." They daydream. They play. They laze about. An author confided after every large project, he enters a lengthy torpor:

> I sleep extra hours each night and walk by the beach. Just when I think I'll never write another line again or that I'm becoming an eggplant, I'm off and running again.

Skillful solution-finders invent, reinvent and juggle every facet of their operation to obtain their ideal working arrangements. Sports, leisure time, or meditative disciplines give them insight. One CEO recently visited Japan with two trusted business colleagues and for several days he toured ancient Japanese temples. Another executive took time out of her busy month to spend a week in Santa Fe with close friends. They visited art stores, rested in the sun, and explored new business plans. A friend turns her weekend—and home—into an occasional health spa. A graduate student told me he is constructing a path in his garden—digging it and bricklaying each morning—as his metaphor for life.

Figuring-out skills transform us into researchers. We don't just swallow traditional, self-help advice. We figure out when rest, play or more structured, routine work is in order. This too requires self-awareness and prudent, low-risk practice. An actor summarized it like this:

There is a precision in life that is sheer poetry, knowing when to make your move, knowing when to get in, and when to get out, and how and when to say your piece.[16]

Typically, if we want to do something new—lose weight, stop smoking, go to college, quit college, change jobs, start a business— the world discourages us. Conventional wisdom says, *"Don't do it. You can't do it. Stay safe."* Our best friends may feel threatened by what they call our unreasonableness. In this matter of "figuring out" what to do when we don't know, people who overcome physical ailments can be excellent guides about finding answers.

Two years ago an acquaintance learned she had breast cancer and faced the trauma of trying to heal within the bounds of traditional medicine. She had to reconcile her usually accommodating disposition with the negative, dehumanizing, and authoritarian treatment she received from doctors. Against their advice, she researched what recovery entailed. The medical establishment discouraged her independence. Despite criticism, she obtained the most up-to-date research findings, supportive audiotapes, and groups for positive uplift and reinforcement while undergoing a mastectomy, then lengthy chemotherapy. Somehow she kept her wits while hearing both old wives' tales and stories about radically new treatments. Her husband became her nutritional detective, unearthing enough helpful data about foods, supplements, and cancer prevention (which he now could use to write a book).

Today, three years later, my acquaintance is well. She's made numerous lifestyle changes: sold her business, revised her diet and many friendships. Her heroic ability to stay sane and care for herself during her treatment was bolstered by the self-belief: *"I can find the answers I need to survive."*

## *"I'm an Incorrigible Experimenter"*

Perhaps our most critically helpful *self*-bias is the notion that we can experiment our way into needed knowledge (or skills). Capable entrepreneurs are like master artists who assume responsibility for the entirety of their ambitions. One young Ph.D. candidate in a course I was teaching argued persuasively that true business success entails *using*—rather than avoiding—errors. He proposed that leadership is *power* to endure an ongoing quest for information or influence (as in Edison's ten thousand tries at an invention), not just actual triumphs like making profits or achieving stated objectives.

We mature entrepreneurially as we test ourselves concretely against life's challenges. *Practice* builds skill. I've heard golfers and tennis players say, "The harder I practice, the luckier my game gets." Hopefully, in terms of "figuring out" a life's work, our practice will involve experimenting with *low-risk* prototypes of what's wanted so that we won't shoot ourselves in the foot with our good intentions or enthusiasms.[17]

I've suggested that people as dissimilar as Mother Teresa or Margaret Mead could teach entrepreneuring skills to industry leaders. For both of these women work is a vocation. Almost anything we do can be a vocation, as an incident in the life of

Frances Willard, a charismatic, nineteenth-century feminist, illustrates. In her fifties and in poor health, Willard's doctor advised her to take regular exercise in fresh air. Willard chose to ride a bicycle against family wishes (and despite the fact that women in her time were "not allowed" on bikes in public). Her motto was *do everything.*

Riding the bike became Willard's learning experiment, her "wheel within a wheel" of lessons, and it taught her to be fully human, which is *the* lesson behind every vocation. Willard's account (written nearly one hundred years ago) beautifully expresses how *any* experience is instructive if we appreciate its layers of learning:

> Once, when I grew somewhat discouraged and said that I had made no progress . . . my teacher [said] that it was just so when she learned: there were growing days and stationary days, and she had always noticed that just after one of these last dull, depressing, and dubious intervals she seemed to get an uplift and went ahead better than ever. It was like a spurt in rowing. This [is] the law of progress in everything we do; it moves along a spiral rather than a perpendicular; we seem to be actually going out of the way and yet it turns out that we were really moving upward all the time.[18]

*Any* new venture can help us understand what, as particular persons, we require in novel circumstances. Most of us would be better innovators if, like Willard, we weren't afraid of looking foolish.

## "I've Escaped the Perfectionist's Trap"

Three interrelated, holistic factors seem requisite to figuring-out skill:

- *positive self-valuation* (i.e., self-trust, self-esteem, self-regard, etc.)

- *learning resourcefulness* (i.e., the ability to *use* or leverage knowledge to learn more in novel areas)

- *growth toward independence* (i.e., movement toward healthy autonomy).[19]

When we care inordinately what others say, when we dwell excessively on what might go wrong, or yearn for advice or praise from those we consider our "superiors," we harm ourselves. Here, again, we divide our own attention. If we've been impaired or hurt as children and grow up loathing ourselves or think we can't make it, then these thoughts create confusion about doing the simplest things.

I know young fast-track executives whose innovative skills are trained out of them. For example, their managers demand they rehearse their staff presentations over and over until these are flawless—and dry as dust. Most arrange it so that when they finally do stand up to speak, they can hide behind flip-charts or audiovisual paraphernalia. They turn off all the lights and, pointer in hand, address their audiences in the dark, with all spontaneity and novelty drained from their talk. They read preapproved texts or recite their notes from memory. Good humor, the chance remark, an improvised idea are considered poor form. Every move is heavily scripted in advance, so as not to offend a given norm.

Rehearsal aimed at a flawless presentation is not wrong—all good theater (and, at times, that's precisely what business is) proceeds in much this way. What damages both individual and corporate creativity is that impressionable executives are programmed to stifle spontaneity in *all* group meetings, including team planning, when fresh, innovative responses are desperately wanted. Fear of looking foolish, anxiety about being chastised by a superior or vilified behind our back impede figuring-out skills. Our elders controlled us by intimidation when we were young. Only the strongest egos escape the trap of perfectionism. To solve problems successfully, you must *believe* you can, must feel capable enough to improvise. Yet too many adults have been schooled away from their ability to experiment freely.

A freelance publicist (and a grand entrepreneur) who I'll call Nora said her parents taught her that she didn't *have* to have a traditional job or worry about fitting artificial norms:

> If my father didn't like a job, he'd say, "To hell with it, I'll get another." My mother never complained about these risks, never whined, "But what about the children?"
>
> I went to seven schools in twelve years. If you're forced into significant changes, you usually make it work. By my senior year in high school I realized that in certain towns I'd never be popular. I was an outcast in Chicago, but a tremendous hit in Dallas. As an adult I make sure things fit. I have a gut feel for places and people, too, and this is an obvious advantage in business.

Nora's parents never criticized her, and raised her with clear and noble standards:

> My mother is fabulous. To this day she's never asked, "Why aren't you married?" She didn't marry until her mid-thirties. She'd been a freelance reporter and fashion designer and explored her world liberally before marrying. My family's full of atypical women. They say, "Go for it!" My ninety-year-old aunt was a missionary, and there were many other amazing, bright women floating in and out of our home. I wanted my life to be at least as interesting as this. No one ever said, "You're a girl and can't do that."

Compare Nora's positive self-biases with those of equally intelligent people you may know who were wounded in childhood by harshly judgmental parents. How can one build a truly rich life without correcting the inevitable damage? For example, a bright, physically healthy fifty-year-old—rebuffed when young by his father, whom he adored—is now bowled over by what he perceives as iron-clad limitations:

> I live on less than $1,000 a month, but pay rent of over $650. I can't find a proper job—one I like. So you see my problem. I don't know where to begin to break out or how to re-do my circumstances. Can you help?

Answers *are* elusive if we lack positive self-value, learning resourcefulness, and a love of independence. Here's when therapy —at the minimum a wholesome support group—seems in order. Without robust *self*-worth, how can we command our mind to organize a business, design a marketing strategy, figure out what risks to take or avoid? Lacking confidence, the most basic daily questions can seem like puzzles of advanced trigonometry. It's not enough to "feel good" about oneself—one eventually must demonstrate one's own competence and power in the real world. Evaluate yourself in this matter with a few general questions:

- How do I *treat* myself after making an understandable but embarrassing mistake?

- To what extent does my fear of looking foolish or being criticized prevent me from trying my hand at hobbies, community involvement, or part-time freelance work?

- If I'm required to give a presentation or state my position in a highly judgmental atmosphere, how *clear-minded* or *sharply focused* am I?

- What early hurts or criticisms may still haunt me, making it difficult for me to solve problems? Might my own anger or resentments (at old injuries) be holding me back?

Note that these inquiries relate to behaviors, not merely to feelings. Figuring-out skill comes from employing your mind's innate, majestic faculties artfully.

# Start on the Ground Floor

Figuring out what to do when we don't know is often most perplexing when we're *emotionally* invested in a matter. We may have several talents and can't decide which one we'd love to use most. Indecision keeps us stuck. At such times, I envision creating solutions as an architecture. Think of building a solid foundation from, say, your dominant skill (the one that could produce a reliable income). Imagine this primary talent as your "first floor." Then, off-shoot (or secondary) talents become "stairs" leading to the next floors you'd like to reach: a desired lifestyle, a novel project, or working conditions. Salespersons with a flair for drama may turn their primary skill (selling) into secondary ones (e.g., mass communication or entertaining) by transitioning into television sales for optimal fun or income—*after* having worked (for decades sometimes) in real estate, automobile, or retail sales (their foundation, first floor). The glitz comes later as they figure out how to diversify their talents and build the larger, more expansive life they want.*

A friend who I'll call "William" figured out his optimal career independently. William worked for an airlines company as a reservations agent. What began as a short-term job nearly turned into his existence. After seven years, William knew he didn't want to spend his entire life behind a reservations desk. He felt he'd be good at work he enjoyed. But, perhaps like you, William had numerous interests and couldn't readily identify his *vocation.* So, he devised what he calls a "backwards technique." Rather than

---

*For an illustration of this "building" process, scan Alona Wartofsky's article ("The Thangs," *Washington City Paper,* June 19, 1993) about how Anita Brown (founder of *It's A D.C. Thang*) created numerous businesses, using *each* venture to figure out viable ways to serve her interests and her community. Currently, her original T-shirts "celebrate growing up black in D.C."

attempting to fit into a job based on title or occupational testing, William first compiled a list of all the qualities he liked in work:

> I kept a running log of work elements that were important to me. I wanted to work anywhere, not be stuck in one location. I wanted to work for myself. I wanted concrete outcomes from my labors, tangible results—and a process that had a finite beginning, a middle, and an end. I wanted to deal with people sometimes, not *all* the time, and to work outdoors once in a while. I gathered a long list of such qualities and thought "backwards": I tried to name jobs I could do that had these characteristics. And actually came up with one!

What did William ultimately do? Why he applied for, and got, a scholarship to Harvard where he studied architecture for the requisite five years. Today he runs his own small design firm.

*Try William's method:*
1. For a week or more (without censoring yourself) list all the desirable *qualities* of the tasks, jobs, or processess of work you enjoy. (Add to your list as your memories and experience remind you of what you prefer or do well.)
2. Adjust your list over time. Review what you've written. Then, "thinking backwards," name the occupations that may offer some elements you've listed.

*Then try this:*
1. For a week or more, identify a few *tasks* that, when you do them, cause you to forget time and space: You begin the thing early on Saturday morning and suddenly, it's evening.
2. List the things *others* say you do well, that you also enjoy and feel *competent* doing (as if an inner intelligence is working

with, through, or *for* you, enabling you to go on automatic pilot).

3. Now "thinking backwards," name a few more jobs or occupations that offer you a chance to do these activities. Then imagine ways of *making money* at your preferred tasks.

## Evaluate Your Readiness

Pay attention to the *world* of work you wish to enter. Watch the nightly news or read the business weeklies to see who's earning money doing what you'd love to do. The current universe of occupational options is boundless. People work from home, minivans, or hotel rooms. For now, consider your self-biases. The more *yeses* you can honestly answer to the following self-assessment inquiry, the higher your comfort level when figuring-out solutions.

- *I have what it takes to "get real," to be tangibly accomplished in the real world.*

- *I create a reasonable fit between my own interests and the needs of the marketplace.*

- *I am an active solution-finder.*

- *I possess good figuring-out skills (even when I don't know "how" to do something, deep down, I know I'll figure it out eventually).*

- *I am an incorrigible experimenter. I enjoy the climb up the mountain-of-discovery (as well as the satisfaction of reaching its pinnacle).*

- *My* actions *demonstrate I trust myself to figure out life's puzzles; my* outcomes *demonstrate others trust me.*

- *I generally enjoy the messy, meandering nature of creative problem-solving: I use both intuitive and rational (logical) means to solve problems. For the most part, I possess productive self-beliefs; I like myself and my behaviors show it.*

· *For me, there's usually a thin line between* play *and* solution-finding.

· *I tolerate, indeed invite, "disorder"—the chaos of change—as one of my primary mechanisms for growth.*

Exercise your *positive* imagination when reviewing your self-beliefs. When are you most *resourceful*? What do you think of yourself then? How do you operate then? Activate your own "successful thinking" methods, using your creative strengths to figure out what else you need.

Some people create imaginary "committees" in their minds to talk to and get direction. Many use brainstorming sessions to bounce ideas off others. Others visualize themselves in parks, wilderness settings, or see themselves meeting gurus who bestow needed answers. Read up on such techniques.[20, 21, 22]

Think back over your significant challenges. *What typically works for you?* Identify the obstacles you've surmounted independently by using your wits. What did you learn about "getting real"? Observe your self-supportive figuring-out style. Success breeds success. Attend to your mind's most joyful, effective discovery process. Bolster the self-beliefs that add confidence, lucidity, and tenacity to your efforts. You'll get more of what you notice, so heed whatever gives you wisdom.

## A SUMMARY STRATEGY

A CPA wanted to be a publicist but lacked experience. He thought, *"If I could just start someplace—whether I'm paid or not—I'll learn some of what I need to know."*

He volunteered to promote an event for his church. The

attendance was better than anyone expected. He received much recognition and many other requests for his talents. His hunch—to take one, concrete step in the direction of his goals—paid off.

*You learn by doing.* Start small in a low risk arena, and stay objectively alert to every bit of feedback.

*Try This:*
On a clean sheet of paper, *define the vocational territory you want to enter.* Use your dictionary. Be as clear as possible. Don't simply say, *"I want to consult."* Expand on that—What kind of consultant? Where? When? For whom? Why?

Now without censoring yourself, quickly *list fifty low-risk, seemingly inconsequential, practical actions you could take to visit—or enter—that "land"* (e.g., attend another consultant's course; read about the topic; interview similar consulting firms, etc.).

Finally, select three steps you're *willing* to take to explore the territory you want to inhabit. Reflect frequently on Alan Lakein's rule for time management:

> You cannot *do* a goal . . . you can [only] do an activity. Activities are steps along the way to a goal . . . And don't let fear bother you that once you list an activity you'll have to do it. No one is going to force you to do it . . .[23]

# CHAPTER 5

# Risk-Taking Effectiveness

> *Before striding recklessly out on the gangplanks of*
> *enterprise, assess your judgment: Have your*
> *previous, calculated choices worked out to your and*
> *other's advantage . . . ? Risk-taking is like gaining*
> *fluency in a foreign language. It involves practice*
> *(not hit-or-miss impulsivity), degrees of complexity,*
> *and hierarchies of mastery.*

R isk is defined as exposure to chance of loss or injury. To stretch into the potentials of our growth or an untried effort, we need proper timing, good judgment—real discernment of what hunches or trends to follow—and an ability to improvise when needed. These are but some ingredients of effective risk-taking. We take risks when attempting anything new, as you know if you've ever said hello to a stranger or traveled to a foreign country alone.

The anxious hold back. They realize, if dimly, that their own confusion, ineptness, or indecisiveness causes unhappiness. In retrospect, they voice sharp regret: "How I wish I had taken advantage of that opportunity when it came up. If only I'd done that years ago."

Dr. Stanley Coopersmith's pioneering research on gifted, creative persons suggests that avoiding risks limits personal growth, yet "many of those who seek the aid of a counselor want someone else to decide for them and to convince them that they can succeed in some specific vocation."[1]

We often measure our effectiveness as *persons* by our risk-taking results. The poorer our judgment in major decision areas, the less we trust ourselves to improvise or choose next time. We all know at least one person whose relationships, health, or career were damaged by a risk and whose self-esteem subsequently plummeted. Therefore, part of creating work involves establishing a solid foundation of chance-taking skills. The story of Judy and Colleen, two close friends who took a chance on each other, may prove useful. They explain that a history of good judgment calls furthers business success. Lacking this, practice in *low* risks is needed before undertaking high risks.

# The Story of Judy and Colleen

Judy and Colleen met years before establishing their partnership, when Judy worked for Colleen in a property management firm. Judy described that relationship:

> We always talked about how great it might be to do things on our own—to use our experience in our *own* business. We continually brainstormed—exploring those things we enjoyed and could do well. Suddenly a year later we heard of a small office-service business for sale, exactly what we wanted. We risked our friendship and our financial security. All our friends and family gave us similar advice: "Never go into business with a friend." But we did.

Colleen remembers hearing much the same counsel:

> Basically, everyone we knew advised, "Don't do it." As we got close to deciding, my head said, "It's a good thing," but my

stomach was in knots. Then, the day after deciding to buy the business, I felt fine—totally free. When it came down to the wire, we didn't even discuss our final decision with our spouses. We just sat here, talking to the seller and then together, on the spot, we decided yes, we'd buy the business.

Before striding recklessly out on the gangplanks of business, assess your judgment calls: Have your previous, calculated choices worked out to your and others' advantage? Are you someone who works hard to make your decisions succeed? Risk-taking is no different than talking, walking, or gaining fluency in a foreign language. Each involves degrees of complexity, practice, and eventually hierarchies of mastery.

When evaluating ourselves, we should recall both failures and successes. Lateral thinking expert Dr. Edward deBono suggests that when business outcomes sour, one measure of self-worth becomes the way we extricate ourselves from the crisis. He cites a wealthy real estate magnate who calls this "wriggling": "It's not all success . . . you don't always come out ahead. But you must handle it. You wriggle. You get off the hook the best you can!"[2]

We build wriggling dexterity variously, and over time. In our previous chapter we saw that Shanalei was solving problems early, at sixteen: "I didn't want to live by the decisions [my mother] made—I didn't like what I saw her doing." She trusted her own choices. Don cultivated his risk-taking skill *years* before founding his sole proprietorship, longer still before he sold it to raise tuition money for college. Colleen and her husband were youthful adventurers, "the first in our family to leave home." They toured the U.S. on their own when fresh out of college. Their nomadic life (perhaps their innate self- and world-view) provided a foundation for their current business philosophy: *"Life is an adventure. You learn from everything."*

Judy feels sufficiently mature to take risks. She's been around business long enough to know when her impulses are reliable. Judy assessed her current business risk *before* taking it:

We never conceived of our venture as a risk to our relationship. We complement one another. Colleen loves to negotiate; I hate that. I like detailed work, and she prefers dealing with the public. The day-to-day tasks naturally separated without fuss or discussion. Then there was the money. Potentially, finances interfere with both friendship and achievement. We just said, "Let's get the business going and not nitpick about the money." We weren't that concerned about money. Sure, this was a gamble but not one with high stakes. I've had enough experience to know when I can say, "Let's just do it." I felt things would be fine, and they are.

Colleen's thinking ran along much the same lines:

We figured that we got along extremely well, and there was simply no reason why we couldn't work things out. The only thing that's changed is that, now, we don't socialize much. That seems natural. After spending every single day together in such close quarters, we thought, "Enough's enough." A certain level of maturity is needed for this sort of arrangement, and probably we have that. Financially, we're making a go of this, and our friendship is just as solid, if not more so, than before.

These two have *learned* to plumb their inner depths despite unknowns. So has Shanalei:

I assess the chances for success by asking myself, "If I take this risk, what do I have to lose?" I look at probable benefits of a choice using a weighing process—almost like Ben Franklin's pro/con list: I write down best/worst case scenarios. If I'm unwilling to live with a large negative possibility, then I'll pass.

Mostly, I find little to lose. In starting my home business, I could have lost money but felt that was replaceable. I can always make it again.

Few effective entrepreneurs impetuously leap into uncharted regions; few practice brinkmanship.

When I was little, my father—an entrepreneur if there ever was one—taught me about driving. Because he spoke on many levels (e.g., parental, practical, philosophical), his lessons transcended any one topic. For instance, once he discussed taking risks while teaching me to pass a car on the open highway:

> Always look far, far beyond the car ahead of you before driving around it. If you see another vehicle coming at you, stay where you are. Calculate its speed—make sure you have room and acceleration enough to pass safely. If it's foggy and you're not sure, don't try just yet. Keep alert. Eventually you'll spot the opening you need. Then, just glide on out there and make your move.

To this day, I use that imagery and his rule of thumb to stay alert. So can you. Wait for the safe opening *you* require before taking your risks. Don't listen to others who tell you, "Now its safe." Use your own powers of observation, your own intuitive and rational forces. You need speed and power and "room enough to pass." Unless you have a death wish, it's to your advantage to have a clear sign of where you're headed before you make your moves. True entrepreneurs love movement, but not danger. They take pains to minimize losses and chaos.

## Minimizing Chaos by "Hearing" Ourselves

You improve your "wriggling" I.Q. by first cutting your teeth on the subjective, soft variables of risk-taking. For instance, you can minimize emotional turbulence and outer chaos by learning to *hear* your ambition, frustrations, or conflicts. Much of what may now seem risky becomes instinctive—necessary to sustain well being—*if* we are healthy enough to accept our vocational urges. That sounds easier than it is.

Facing our authenticity seems one of our greatest fears. Jungian analyst Florida Scott-Maxwell surveys this dread from her octogenarian's perspective:

> The ordeal of being true to your own inner way must stand high in the list of ordeals. It is like being in the power of someone you cannot reach, know, or move, but who never lets you go; . . . Precious beyond valuing as the individual is, his fate is feared and avoided. Many do have to endure a minute degree of uniqueness, just enough to make them slightly immune from the infection of the crowd, but natural people avoid it. They obey for comfort's sake the instinct that warns, "Say yes, don't differ, it's not safe." It's not easy to be sure that being yourself is worth the trouble, but we do know it's our sacred duty.[3]

One way to improve *vocational* risk-taking is by differentiating between our *compulsion* to do things and the quieter, sweeter press of our still, small voice. This quieter impulse is distinctly spiritual. It tells us to reach for the "good life" which, as theologian Paul Tillich writes, is "life, willing to surpass itself." Perhaps that urge appears in what Emerson called "divine discontent." To create the work you want, you must hear your uniqueness calling, and then practice *being* yourself within the context of your present day life.

During a recent David Frost interview with Isaac Stern, the famed violinist generously disclosed his ambition to instill in his protégés the *ability to hear themselves*. Stern hopes students will "experience what they want—*before* playing it—to experience, then express themselves as whole and independent persons." Stern suggests this self-instruction is "a great teaching."[4] Similarly, the best business risk-takers usually *hear* themselves before venturing forth.

Judy's and Colleen's stories illustrate what this hearing-of-self might entail. Each *heard* herself wanting to preserve a friendship. The value of friendship became an important component of their business-design.* Judy's remark, "We just got the business going first and didn't want to nitpick about the money," suggests that their business plans and their format maximized elasticity. They allowed themselves plenty of room to "wriggle," to experiment with whatever happened.

As noted, when Colleen considered the financial risks, she realized she'd always been an adventurer:

> My husband and I have traveled extensively. Our idea is, "What can we lose?" . . . Our attitude is, "We can always learn something." Life is definitely a learning experience. However, we're not gamblers. We know we can use everything we've discovered in our next trip or enterprise, even if we have to turn around and begin again.

Traveling gave the couple room to fail, ways to learn how to "wriggle." George Burns, one of my favorite senior humorists, credits vaudeville for giving him and his comedienne wife, Gracie Allen, a place to experiment, to learn from their mistakes. We, too, need spaces in which to fail safely, to monitor our performance, to correct and improve ourselves. Practicing these skills, we reconfigure "how" to do all manner of things. Before creating a new venture, consider creating a trial-and-error zone that readies you for the work and life you desire. If you've never considered this, if the notion of *practicing* low risks is novel to you, find a "pro" you trust and discuss such ideas before starting.

Effective risk-takers, like gifted violinists, apparently tune in to and *hear* their hesitation or their inner prompts to move forward. Recalling Isaac Stern's remark, "we give out of our fullness of

---

*For a helpful look at how a corporation integrates *values* into its operating systems, see Tom Chappell's *The Soul of a Business* (Bantam Books).

heart, not our tensions,"[5] makes me suggest that this fullness involves our finest inner faculties which should serve our art of enterprise, whatever we decide it should be.

## Minimize Errors by Identifying Skills

Just as Isaac Stern's goal is to encourage inward listening in his master students, mine is to fine tune your sensitivity to your trustworthy instincts. How might you experience *what* you want before risking all for it? Who—or what—might help you clarify your various subtleties of self, or inner longings, so that you hear what you're about in a way that enhances awareness and a more fluid action pattern? To advance wholesomely, to further your authentic purposes, a repertoire of solid risk skills is needed. Moreover, self-assessment is a precursor to building such skills.

In late 1992, I met with about a hundred executives in a university workshop to explore the relationship between risk-taking and leadership. The majority admitted they pressured themselves into decisions when dealing with high risks. Some believed they *had* to please everyone—both management and employee groups. They felt overly cautious and conservative. Others, who knew better, tried to rescue or protect staff members. As a group, these business people were exceptionally self-aware. They knew what they ideally wanted but saw themselves fettered by worry and holding back when taking eventful risks. Most felt their leadership would improve if they stopped *overthinking* and *overanalyzing* matters—in other words, if they weren't so afraid of failing.

The most common "needs to improve" areas were:

- *to create new "mental tapes" relative to taking normal risks,*

- *to speed up decision-making (many felt they were inordinately slow in judging the merits of new directions or policies),*

117

- *to become more confident, gain spontaneity, to let go of the need to control outcomes,*

- *to learn from fears or errors and move beyond these,*

- *to clearly articulate and understand their goals.*

It is likely that many of these executives are too self-critical. After all, they have been successful because of their reliably good judgment. We do not want people in power, responsible for the welfare of multiple others, to be cavalier in taking risks. Still, almost all of us can and should improve our risk-taking acumen. We do this most easily by first factoring out the precise skills involved, and then, considering our strengths and weaknesses, mapping out an intelligent plan to improve in specific areas.

Effective risk-taking gives us choice-making *artistry:* We become more like master violinists, poets, or fine athletes with respect to daily decisions. Otherwise we remain like brutes or machines. As the Zen saying goes, we should respond *instinctively* to events "in the spirit of a person trying to extinguish a blaze from his hair."[6] Students of Zen philosophy spend years meditating in hopes of elevating their actions to this spiritually gifted level of alacrity. They strive to live intimately in the moment, instead of fragmenting their attention with cerebral abstractions about what they "should" or "must" do. I've proposed a learn-by-doing method wherein we use *low-risk* facsimiles to gain "wriggling dexterity" and good judgment. Whatever self-improvement route you choose, you'll need discernment to balance your desire for achievement or growth against the hazards your passions could invite. Inward listening creates spaces—or ways—to fail safely and develops discernment—*if* you pay attention to the data in the feedback. In part, this includes hearing what your intellect says you "should" do while sensitizing yourself to the values and vocation in your heart.

## "Belly Faith" vs. "Head Faith"

The internationally renowned Korean pastor, Dr. Paul Yonggi Cho heads the world's largest church with some half-million to one million members. As a young man, he established it without funds or community support, after being miraculously healed of a terminal illness. Many of Cho's books and lectures talk of bridging the gap between spiritual and worldly attainment. Let me try to express one of his principles in my own secular terms:

In one address, Cho delineates the subtle, meticulous nuances of what he calls *belly faith* (perhaps we'd call it a "gut feel"). He differentiates between it and *head faith* (intellectual urging). By *belly faith* Cho means, of course, the guidance of the Holy Spirit (or Rhema, God's word to us, as particular individuals). Cho describes his own disastrous consequences when taking risks driven solely by head faith.

Once, when visiting California, a ministerial colleague persuaded Cho to enter what was then a newly emerging Christian broadcasting field. This sounded logical. His intellect (head faith) urged full speed ahead. Instead of waiting to hear his inner leading, he pressed forth impatiently. Returning to Korea, Cho invested heavily in state-of-the-art engineering equipment, constructing a fine recording studio. When he tried to get broadcasting permits, he was told that there were no available frequencies for his project. Cho maneuvered every way possible yet was blocked at each turn. From that and other experiences, Cho learned to listen carefully to his inmost spirit.[7]

## Inward Listening Makes Good Business Sense

It is intensely pleasurable—exquisite really—to consciously sift through all our inmost subtleties and learn to hear ourselves.

# A Step Ladder of Risk-Taking Skills©

A Chinese proverb says people—like gems—are polished by friction. Scanning the risk-taking levels below, keep in mind this chart is far from exhaustive. Even superior riskers "polish" themselves—grow capably skillful—stepping through the trials and pressures of everyday risks. This means we'll *all* recognize risk-taking weaknesses or spot aspects of ourselves in *each* column.

Search for your *dominant tendencies* (rather than rigidly trying to slot yourself into one of the three categories). High risks (i.e. which call for significant investments of emotion, resources, relationship, etc.) invite the probability of struggle with "below average" tendencies—like overthinking or ignoring the big picture—and do so repeatedly until one moves beyond ineptness. From below-average through superior levels, *some* risk-taking levels include . . .

## BELOW AVERAGE

- generally rigid or scattered; a dysfunctional thinker; needs structured supervision when risking
- easily distracted and unfocused or confused; low to weak mental energy and concentrative powers
- thinks in details: misses big picture
- wants guaranteed outcome, advice, before risk; dislikes visibility when wrong or mistaken and passes the buck to avoid accountability or blames the advice-giver when things don't work
- fears trying—or hearing—new ideas; finds ambiguity threatening and may feel hostile toward pathfinders, the creative, free spirits of the world
- needs dominant others (experts, authority figures, parental types, etc.) to give "how to" advice; drawn to the charismatic pathfinder
- overthinks and overtalks goals as a way of eliciting "don't do it" advice
- may be impulsive at times and at others risk averse (or one of these traits could dominate)
- easily discouraged; finds delays or rejections depressing, quits easily
- judgment history seems faulty; can't seem to evaluate probable consequences; craves the quick-fix solution
- often shoots self in foot with own choices
- timing seems off; in wrong place "at wrong time"

## AVERAGE

- takes calculated risks sparingly, often with anxiety
- distances self from high risks or postpones indefinitely
- reluctant to accept responsibility or accountability for new choices (but likes to take credit when they work)
- takes risks when chips are down but doesn't initiate risks unless forced to
- watches others to see what they do before taking a stand; wonders what people will say *if* s/he missed mark
- *sometimes* evaluates probability of outcomes
- timing is spotty; sometimes good, sometimes "off"
- dislikes uncertainly, prefers the known, the formula, *the* answer
- likes directives: maps, blueprints or "how-to" advice before moving toward abstract goals
- often overlooks the obvious, common-sense option
- plods (instead of dances) toward choices
- good concentrative ability, but may get distracted by complicated variables to the extent of missing the right moment to risk or losing focus

## SUPERIOR

- "fluid" detachment: spontaneous right choice—intellect does not clog action
- high tolerance for ambiguity; transcends "good" or "bad" polarizations
- *generally* gauges probability of outcomes correctly (uses some form of risk analysis for high risks)
- often floats trial balloons before "risking all"
- master strategist; "sees" long-range probabilities; excellent forecaster; intuitive
- blends logical, rational faculties with intuitive powers
- superior history of reliable judgment calls (uncanny "common" sense); hunches usually pay off; good to great street sense
- takes high risks after close scrutiny of variables or consequences
- excellent improviser; thinks on feet; trusts own instincts; uses errors as feedback for next steps
- prefers own answers yet remains open to input from multiple sources; a natural "explorer"
- superior timing; tolerates the tension of delays and uncertainty; focused despite pressure or distractions
- superior risk manager; says "no" to short-term gain to win long-range advantage, protects assets, etc.
- keeps "playing" with solutions; optimistic that answers can be found—in time; patient, persevering
- *uses* errors as feedback on data for moving ahead
- productive self-management: fear, indecision, compulsions are handled—subordinated to overall vision or goal

Doing so, we apply awareness to awareness. With inner and objective eyes we observe our *particular* ground of being. If only dimly, we soon sense what to do next. Yet these understandings are gained only as we "listen" with our *entire* being—without distractions and in stillness.

Inner stillness is perhaps our greatest ally. Gandhi once wrote that this silence brings "the highest potency and is self-acting [power]." Prayer, meditation, reading scripture (which is, to me, alive with silence, embedded with sacred codes about our deepest mind)—even quiet walks on the beach—become *healing* acts. These quiet the world's noises and provide clues about who we are and our healthiest directions.

Confucius taught that to listen in this way is to *fast at the heart:*

> The hearing that is only in the ears is one thing. The hearing of the understanding is another. But the hearing of the spirit is not limited to any one faculty, to the ear, or to the mind. Hence it demands the emptiness of all the faculties. And when the faculties are empty, then the whole being listens. There is then a direct grasp of what is right there before you that can never be heard with the ear or understood with the mind. . . . Fasting of the heart begets [inner unity] and freedom.[8]

When I began my corporate practice, I had a burning wish to create a body of knowledge about robust, creative functioning. I lacked family and business connections. I had little industrial experience and no capital to speak of. However, I felt my understanding of the life-concerns and attributes of the creatively gifted had tangible, universal application. I saw I could express myself along broad, boundless lines and wanted to share my excitement about these themes from what seemed a practical, unorthodox framework. However, before building the life I craved, I invested years readying myself, emptying the faculties, meditating and "listening."

Attending mostly to hunches, I spent nearly three months writing my first business article, then submitted that to a reputable human resource journal that scheduled the piece for publication immediately. Upon its release (six months later) a major newspaper spotlighted my ideas in its Sunday business spread, adding glowing testimonials about the article's wisdoms. The exposure was tremendous. The newspaper acknowledged my corporate expertise in a way no marketing firm could have arranged. The probabilities of such a happening were negligible.

Guided as I was by "belly faith," illogically I *knew* my tiny human resource firm would thrive. But don't ask me how I knew. There is a paper-thin line between this "knowing" and sheer presumption. Therefore, all had best beware—in advance.

# Risk-Taking as Art

No one can give another a formula for risk-taking success. That is why, from the start, I compare this whole topic of creating work to art (neither science nor gambling). I speak a conservative's language: merit, competency, and careful planning count. Taking liberties with the sentiment of one Zen master, "Fundamentally [this living] is a matter of people arriving [at their own conclusions] and finding out for themselves; only then can they talk about it."[9] Being responsible in small matters, drawing our own conclusions about daily choices, we begin to understand through "belly faith" larger, more significant ones. There is, in my mind, no finer way to grow. *We learn gradually, by remaining alert and by doing.*

To enhance your risk-skills, *devise safe arenas* in which you can make mistakes and learn about your choices and yourself. You'd never teach your child to drive during rush hour on a busy thoroughfare, so don't practice your risks on dangerous ground. (I have expounded at length on Positive Structuring method relative to "how" this works![10]) Chapter Three suggested some approaches. Well-supervised adventure excursions, ordinary camping expeditions, and even weekend outings can serve us exactly as vaudeville served George Burns, who used it to learn the ins and outs of show business. I recall one talented secretary who hoped to create her own business but who knew she lacked risk-taking skill. She'd never ridden a bus alone, never visited an urban city by herself. Solo bus and train rides and downtown explorations were her first, small-scale "risks." Every decent teacher recognizes that practice helps us learn anything new: Eventually we must stop intellectualizing and apply ourselves to the tests of life.

Famed educator Maria Montessori explains the goal: Our object is not to learn how to perform a task or fulfill someone else's expectation. Rather, our aim is an inner one:

> Namely, that the [person] train himself to observe; that he be led to make comparisons between objects, to form judgments, to reason and to decide; and *it is in the indefinite repetition of this exercise of attention and of intelligence that a real development ensues.*[*][11]

A couple recounted their strategy to exit the corporate womb. First, they *experimented* with various small home-based businesses. Concurrently, they saved money. Even then, after their lengthy planning phase, only the wife quit her regular job to begin a mail-order business in their basement. She took in typing to make ends meet. That's what *their* trail-and-error, low-risk explorations suggested. Today, four years later, their mail-order business has *just* started sprouting signs of life. The secretarial service is flowering in all directions (including desktop and graphic services). Yet the husband keeps his full-time, corporate position. This couple conservatively engineered a high "wriggling" IQ. Their tactic proves my start-up rules: Begin small. Go slow. Build skill. Deal *meticulously* with your present circumstance and keep refining your strategy.

Iron out the kinks in your attitude (or business) as you go. *Don't take extravagant, largely unnecessary risks*—unless, of course, you're

---

*Author's italics for emphasis.

particularly eager to learn what it means to grow from your mistakes. It is your "indefinite repetition" of *low vulnerability* explorations that improves the risk reflexes and builds "wriggling" dexterity.

While many people seek structured guidelines before committing to a new path, experienced entrepreneurs seem to balance the logic and illogic of their moves. First, they reflect on their previous effectiveness. Judy's remark, "I know myself well enough by now, and I've been around enough start-up ventures to say, 'Let's just do it,'" suggests entrepreneurs may have a success memory. They *feel* their way along much as we might when wandering down a long dark hallway. Second, they do their homework, such as comparing the costs of bank financing versus using their own capital. Effective risk-takers rarely jeopardize their life's security for a short-lived bit of glory.

Prudent risk-taking involves making contingency plans, asking "what if? . . ." and assessing the probability of failure. (This process seems exactly like what we do when passing another car on the freeway.) To evaluate the consequences of our moves strategically, *before* we glide into the unknown is simply sensible. Both Judy and Colleen carefully discussed whether they could live with a worst-case outcome. Colleen decided she wasn't gambling:

> My decision was quite calculated, even though—when push came to shove—I thought, "Well, I'm going for it." Earlier, my husband made spread sheets on various scenarios. We analyzed our worst possibility and felt we could survive that.

Judy's process was virtually identical: She used intuition *and* analysis—the best blend of belly and head faith:

> You never know for sure, so I had my accountant run worst-case numbers for me. Also my husband supported me. Really we weren't gambling the family fortune. With all that information in my back pocket, I finally chose to invest in the

business because I have confidence in what I can do. I know what I'm good at. I trust that.

Most people who are willing to take small, calculated risks soon find they distance themselves from cataclysmic chances. Discernment grows. They wait. They take their sweet time.

Effective risk-takers monitor the potential downside variables before throwing caution, cash reserves, or other resources to the wind. This is why significant choices can be so painful to make and often take so long: Consciously or not, we are considering multiple alternatives at once—weighing one unlike factor against another. This takes its physical toll. Some say they sleep more during critical decision-making times. Others wake up at three in the morning. The greater our conscious, intuitive rapport with our depths, the likelier we'll know, in faith, *what* to do. Some self-help books tell us to sever all our old connections or make decisions boldly despite our fears, so as to commit fully to our new directions. I like golfer Harvey Penick's comment, "When I ask you to take an aspirin, please don't take the whole bottle."[12] A *small,* conscious step toward a sound outcome is often more intelligent than a reckless advance.

## Rigidity as a Barrier

If you believe you *must* act in some predetermined fashion, you're not free to choose. Your intellect fights against you. Of course, if you smell smoke or hear someone yell "fire" in a theater, then your wish to escape becomes paramount: You'll not have time to *think* about what to do. You'll act. But since, even in our era of accelerating change, most decisions are not of an emergency nature, you'll usually have the luxury of at least a bit of time to consider your options. At the same time, *overthinking* stimulates "head faith" and is often as perilous to success as is mindless impulsivity.

Today, most of us have almost too many options. We face numerous, profoundly life-altering choices: Should we relocate? Change careers? Retire early? Should we have a baby? Marry? Divorce? Sell our present home? These endless inquiries assault peace-of-mind. Our jobs also offer unlimited chances for discomfort or failure. A friend runs the benefits department of a multinational firm. He invests enormous sums for his corporation's pension fund, carrying the weight of employees' financial future on his shoulders. He says that at the end of each day that he doesn't want to consider any decision, not even whether to stop for gas: "I go home on automatic pilot and glide home to rest until the next day's frenzied onslaught." My friend is slow-moving and even-tempered. He accepts his need to relax. Someone more rigid might feel guilty about "gliding home to rest," since rigidity carries with it *excessive* purposefulness.

Author Dr. David Shapiro proposes that when our choices are motivated by neurotic rigidity, we are rarely fluid. We then second-guess ourselves, fret about what others might say or want, and ignore our positive instinctive drives—our "belly faith." Instead of living spontaneously, we project our fantasy of duty outward, substituting authoritarian *self*-pressure for robust free choices. We feel *"I should"* or *"I must"* improve, read a book, change jobs, grow, open a business, move, or invest money. Thus, our personal imperatives are muddied to such an extent that either we can't act or we force ourselves to act. Only one option is acceptable to *us*. Shapiro writes that when ruled by compulsions, we say,

> "I must get the fence painted this weekend!" as though referring to some objective necessity, or "I really want to read that book!" . . . as one would if determined to overcome some external obstacle. But there is no compelling objective necessity or external obstacle. The urgent tone typical of these declarations, their language of will and resolve . . . is directed at the speaker himself, at his own resistance or disinclination. That tone makes it clear that the meaning and experience of

such declarations is the imperative, "I should!" [These sentiments] are reminders of duty—directives, admonitions, or reproaches in the manner of a superior addressing a subordinate.[13]

The "should" imperative causes procrastination. We may sense what we want, but we *think* we must do otherwise. Either we press forward with "excessive purposefulness," or get confused. One man wrote that he immobilized himself by intense self-pressure. He simply *could not* choose what he most wanted. He felt such resistance that, despite therapy, he was tortured with indecision:

> My stuckness hurts me and others. Family members are inconvenienced by my lack of enthusiasm. They want to take my wishes into consideration when making their own plans. But I lack direction. I want to be spontaneous but weep in despair because I can't even buy a book [on a subject I value] without the pain of thinking "I must" do this.

Here's when reflective disciplines like yoga, meditation, or nature outings nicely augment therapy—especially when the latter seems an insufficient help. It helps to get "out of our minds," to stimulate and hear our body's memory of who we are at our best. Gentle, noncompetitive disciplines can correct our tendency to pressure ourselves. People who overintellectualize everything report that a walk on the beach helps them "rest" into their feelings or intuitions. Hard physical labor (gardening, construction projects, even washing a floor or a car) is often an antidote to our artificial "I should/I must" programming.

When I need answers, I prefer to garden or spend time out of doors. A long walk early in the day restores true appreciation for little natural things: fresh air and dawn light, frogs croaking. I find such self-forgetfulness healing. I've adopted a "do less, be more" stance, gleaned from the counsel of the world's great scriptures. All sacred writings urge us to pray, to wait, to take time to hear our highest inmost wisdom—to empty our heart, as the Buddha taught—and discover the truth which, even now, awaits us.

As we familiarize ourselves with our quiet inner world, we somehow relax into ourselves, accept ourselves for who and what we are. Then, what once seemed an alien act—e.g., sitting in silence, watching a sunrise, declining some pointless activity—becomes automatic, necessary—like breathing.

# Learning from Errors:
# The "Avoiding Danger" Trap

You can't reach your vocational goals without greeting some unknowns. Avoiding risks *is* a huge trap. Sometimes, to paraphrase Erich Fromm, we hurt because we want what isn't very good for us. Rigid people find it almost impossible to admit this or learn from mistakes. They forfeit growth because taking a risk and possibly making an error is potentially humiliating. Healthy choosers (mostly good risk-takers) use every experience—even "mistakes"—to learn what's needed. The next time, they come closer to actualizing their objective. An accomplished banker friend routinely asks himself *and* his management team, "What's our take-away (i.e., what did we learn) from this month's experiences?" To him, both advances and setbacks yield rich information for personal and business growth.

Another entrepreneur started and ran a publishing venture with only moderate success for a few years. He later dissolved his firm, accepting a managerial position in a large traditional corporation. When his publishing efforts came to a natural conclusion, he realized he "wanted a regular job." Self-employment brought him to his next step, taught him he needed wider responsibilities:

> I wouldn't have had enough confidence to accept this managerial position if I hadn't experienced the ups and downs of my

own business. Now I'm prepared to manage a large enterprise and other people. I couldn't have done that before.

What *looks* like a setback is a neutral happening. A move from self-employment to corporate employment is just an event. *We* stamp our emotions and verdict on things. Some people experience deep depression when leaving one venture for another. Others rejoice. Individuals (or whole groups) set themselves up for failure if they cannot reconcile change, errors, or disappointment with their definition of success. Here, entrepreneur Paul Hawkens's philosophy seems sound:

> If you conceive and create a business where everything has to go right, one error, one mishap, can ruin a lot of good work. If you conceive a business where twenty serious mistakes could occur, and then you create safeguards to deal with some or most of these possibilities, you are creating a survivor. In the beginning, survival is more important than success. Survival is staying on the field, playing the game, learning the rules, and beginning to grow.[14]

Our own beliefs create inner turmoil or harmony and lifelong learning. *If* we can assimilate every event as instruction, *nothing* is wasted, no experience is for naught.

Consider this matter of risk and rigidity. Enroll in supportive adult education programs or talk with trusted colleagues about their risk patterns. Increase personal accountability for your own creative initiatives. Innovate conservatively, then monitor and evaluate your risks in "unimportant" realms as discussed. Use your low-risk results as feedback to guide you further. Reviewing this chapter's ideas, appraise yourself:

- *How well do I minimize chaos by listening inwardly?*

- *What's my attitude about learning from everything?*

- *What risk-taking habits have worked for me in the past?*

- *What's my "wriggling" I.Q.?*

- *What* specific skills *might extend my own risk-taking effectiveness?*

- *What do I tell myself about experimenting, mistakes, and my own hesitancies?*

- *How might "I should/I must" beliefs block my own spontaneity?*

- *How well do I distinguish between my gut feel and compulsive self-pressure?*

Reflect frequently on Helen Keller's practical insight: "Avoiding danger is no safer in the long run than outright exposure; the fearful are caught as often as the bold." You'll soon realize that it's *impossible* to grow without some self-testing and some risk. Keller seems to have followed the biblical precept: "If you try to save your life, you lose it." You can too.

## A SUMMARY STRATEGY

I once hired a strategic planning expert (at around $300 an hour) to advise me how to merge my writing and business interests. He told me to consider writing a hobby, adding there were no fiscal benefits to my objective. I met with him only that once and have worked hard since then to erase all memory of his counsel from my mind.

Be careful whose advice you buy or solicit. As Judy and Colleen indicate, you can easily find people everywhere to discourage you—for free.

Before exercising your risk-taking muscles, reflect on your early life. Ask yourself:

- Who taught me how to take risks? What lessons did I learn? What methods of instruction did they use?
- How successful, as chance-takers, were my earliest significant teachers and role models?
- Reviewing my own life's major mistakes, what patterns of choice-making weakness and strength do I detect? (How might these observations direct my current decisions?)

# CHAPTER 6

# A Strategic Outlook

*Without a strategy you remain vulnerable to
marketplace shifts, or your self-sabbotaging inner
forces and oversights. We all take our vocational
twists and turns; we all have shortcomings.
Strategies devise compensating moves for these.*

Creating work requires tactical thinking. For this, we use our
mind as if playing chess or checkers. We "see" the entirety
of our occupation's gameboard (i.e., the universe or variables
of our endeavor) while simultaneously attending to details. A
strategic mind guides us from point A to point B—through the
various junctures and decision stops along the road of creating
work. These points are, of course, subtle and unseen for the most
part, and that's part of the enjoyment.

A man I'll call John turned his hobby into a business. For years
John felt confined to an office while craving more physical activity.
His initial strategy involved sizing up his situation: He had no
dependents, he was debt-free, and his expertise was solid. He felt
his knowledge and technical credibility gave him an easy place to
start. Fortunately, John is conceptual and found a way to mesh his
love of adventure and the outdoors with marketplace realities. For
him, a profitable strategy is market driven. Still, it took John several
years to transform his hobby into a viable enterprise. And, he adds,
"I'm still working at it."

Phil, an equipment engineer, created a consulting business out

133

of his corporate experience, not to change occupations but rather to build what was, for him, a better life:

> I didn't fit into big-company conservatism. I always felt unrecognized, unfulfilled. Next to love—in life *and* work—I value freedom. I continually struggled with conformity issues. I craved autonomy but didn't have it.

Years earlier, a traumatic divorce forced Phil into a self-assessment process. He took stock of how he'd perpetuated an angry game of vilifying others—his boss, his former wife—to skirt responsibility for his own feelings and ambitions. Phil's initial strategy was somewhat less conceptual than John's, perhaps because his transition merely altered, then extended, his existing professional life (i.e., equipment engineering) rather than terminating it. Whereas John had left a corporate profession to create a wholly new enterprise, Phil evolved a business out of a familiar radius of friendships, knowledge, and industrial ties. The personal dimension—not so much the marketplace—demanded his attention at the beginning.

> I first had to elevate myself to the point of feeling entitled to have the life and work I enjoy. Then, my business vision followed. I negotiated an early retirement and a way to work part-time, on contract. My pension and savings provided a fall-back position. I translated my basic nature (my wish to be free, do work I love with people I enjoyed, my desire to add value to others) into a service that people could afford.

One of Phil's most helpful strategies included blending his engineer's fact-gathering training (i.e., his sorting and analyzing tasks) with "hearing and articulating" his feelings. He says, "Analysis can turn into a mind game: If a goal is not what you really want, you stand a risk of hurting yourself in the long run." His strategy was full of common sense.

For years Phil had admired his company's equipment suppliers, realizing they were bright, capable engineers. Now, he cultivated the business side of those friendships, attended trade shows and diligently let his industrial community know of his plans to freelance.

> I just marketed myself informally, honestly. I'd say, "Do you know someone who needs my technical expertise?" Amazingly, large company downsizing has meant the engineering staff is shed first. Full-time engineers are expensive. Today, companies are happy to buy the services they need—from someone like me!

## Climbing Your Vocational Ladder

Transitions like Phil's can take decades, and during this time a decent strategy can carry you through years of emotional or financial fluctuation. Even if you have only a hazy image of what you'll do, your strategy gives you a sort of road map to manifest your vision. Thinking strategically, you'll consider what makes you (or your business) different from competitors or identify your first-year priority activities. A strategy helps you say no to certain offers, while pursuing things that, at first glance, may seem foreign or out of reach. While some people keep their strategies general, others want a detailed outline. This, I suspect, relates more to how we like to use our mind than to anything else.

Much like John, Woody envisioned a radical change in his work *and* his way of life. Yet, perhaps more like Phil, Woody's strategic process grew out of what he knew best—an engineer's planning model. A hazy image of a goal would never suit Woody. He likes structure and precision. Woody likes to hold a tight rein over his high risks. Before describing his strategic methods, let me note that we become adept tacticians as we rid ourselves of unauthentic ambitions. This, as I repeatedly stress, involves our growing whole and developing endeavors that are rightly ours by virtue of our unique disposition and gifts.

Listening to Woody talk, I actually pictured him climbing up a progressively healthier vocational ladder. As you savor his comments, consider the movement of his life *as a whole:* from insecurity toward security; from counterfeit (or survival) work to a search, then to a discovery of genuine vocation; from material to aesthetic, even spiritual, expressions. Woody illustrates how vocation adds a symmetry and balance to our life. It rounds us out as complete persons.

However, don't be surprised if—en route to your authentic vocation—part of your ascent to greater authenticity includes various tumbles. The path of healing embraces much inner work (like dealing with old, untreated pain, loss, or disappointments). Most people who choose to pursue a true vocation spend at least a bit of time in therapy, spiritual direction, or substantive self-study. Growth has its costs.

## Woody's Story

Early money problems separated Woody from his authentic interests. Childhood deprivations and a need for security made Woody originally select what I term a survival profession. Perhaps his experience matches yours:

> I was interested in art, sculpture, building tree houses, being outdoors. But when I was young, money was tight, so I steered myself toward high salaries and an engineering degree. I entered corporate life driven strictly by financial considerations. After eleven years as an engineer, life was simply a conglomeration of things. I drove a BMW. My wife and I owned a beautiful, expensive, bay-view home. We lived the picture-perfect, San Francisco life.

Incrementally, Woody and his wife transformed their affluent, urban San Francisco life into their present simpler one. (Today Woody is a licensed contractor.) Woody applied his meticulous engineering practices to his new objectives.

> I'm a sure-bet person. I plan things systematically so that when I finally do execute my plan, it's a dead-ringer success. I've learned that planning produces the best outcomes. I'm not impulsive. If I am, then nine times out of ten, I'm learning about what I *shouldn't have done.*

> My engineering background taught me to employ an eighteen-month cycle for developing projects. My first transitional step was just to define my goal. This was particularly hard, very time consuming. It took me over two years to get clear about that. I notice this is still evolving. Then I just blocked out the necessities of my path and struggled to describe my desired end point. Basically, I used what's called a Pert Chart: a simple management scheduling system. I outlined the identifiable steps that might take me to my goal and put a time frame around all that. This just involves saying "I'm at A. I want to get to B. What must I do for that to happen? How long will it take? What resources do I need?"

Your strategy will include all the relevancies of your venture, which now you may see only via a screen of desires in your mind. This picturing function (i.e., our mind's eye) lets us imaginatively forecast eventualities, or scrolls us back over the past, to survey our history in like endeavors. Because a strategic outlook is both innocently simple and intricately shrewd, to win at business—in risks, marketing, and strategy—you need a gamesman's skill.

Without a strategy you lay yourself open to attack. At the very least, you remain vulnerable to marketplace shifts or being done in by your own self-sabotaging inner forces. We all take our vocational twists and turns; we all have personal shortcomings. Strategists devise compensating moves for these. A strategy lets us hold onto our vision, keep market trends or customer needs in mind, and not get lost in the details of the trees while ignoring the forest of our enterprise.*

Chess authorities I. A. Horowitz and Fred Reinfeld believe that the alertness required for championship chess involves "steady, grueling practice and study."[1] Their prescription should hearten, not discourage, us. With rapt attention, almost everyone can learn almost anything. (The easiest way is to adopt the *mind* of those you would emulate.)

For those lacking conceptualizing skill, a chess player's mind seems of a higher caliber than our usually unaware one. The former is sharply focused, surveys micro and macro events simultaneously, and lifts us above circumstances—i.e., our own little game board of daily problems or adversaries. It formulates protective holding patterns or advantageous avenues of advance. Not surprisingly, to display our full potential, we must be willing explorers of such routes. The vocationally maturing pour themselves into a vital experience of life. Learning becomes lifelong. Because their learning happens primarily as a result of their natural bent (and authentic focus), it is also pleasurable.[2]

Need I add that this process of strategic-conceptualization invites transcendence, the peak experience born of self-forgetful-ness? Now our mind is progressively organized by innate fascina-tions and the limitless possibilities of existence. This, then, gives us the same "rapt attention" chess players need for their game's strategic sight. To develop this mind, somehow we must outgrow fear; not suppress it, not deny it, but quiet its voice and logic. At least that's been my experience. Paraphrasing the metaphysician Bicknell Young, our personal unfolding involves an uninterrupted flow of needed ideas (or things). These come as we experience ourselves as pure Being. Of course, as scripture warns, fear *is* the great concealer, the hinderer. It separates us from the lucidity of our own creative intelligence.

---

*For more specific strategic help, read some of the books discussed in the Afterword.

Whenever I face demoralizing circumstances, I skirt—or manage—these by transcending fear, not by tangling with it. I find prayer and silence centering. I meditate on a verse or line of scripture or talk with a friend who's firm and loving enough to straighten out my thinking or who reminds me of my faith. All these acts revive my objective, strategic forces. For me, it's the *coupling* of positive faith and strategic thinking that produces viable long-term solutions. *These* answers change things, shift my mind beneficently in a way that calms or alters negative conditions.

To move beyond constricting beliefs about what can (or can't) be done, we need to notice that beliefs—not conditions—enslave us and turn problems into gods. All sorts of impairments lessen as we cultivate strategic brightness.

Strategic thinking adds two important perspectives, as the stories in this chapter illustrate. In futurist Alvin Toffler's dialect, one "formulates straight-line strategies for normal events; the other thinks in non-linear discontinuous terms."[3]

To put it simply, it's a blend of logic and illogic—some might say our left brain *and* our right—that "creates work." We must pay attention to both "big picture" *and* subtle nuances in surroundings and relationships. These factors all have business consequences. We may set up our own defeat by constant worry or obvious oversights. Yet, at the Being level of vocation, we are organically integrated with our work, uniquely suited to both large and little issues. This must be why some people make what they do look easy: Comparatively speaking, for them, it *is* easy: Their work fits them like good shoes the feet.

Starting a game of chess or opening a business requires strong self-protective moves. Experts agree: Your first task involves translating your overall vision into marketplace benefits. This alone is strategic. Like all master players, you'll need to know before starting out *what* you want to accomplish. The "how" flows from the "what."

Thinking strategically, your mind moves back and forth between your overarching vision and, say, the realities of your financial or customers' needs. Ordinarily, people look to others to tell them how to proceed. But entrepreneurial success requires grappling with an ever-changing flux of independent thinking, interrelationships, and improvisation. Here too a chess analogy describes the mind we need:

> The average player always has an uneasy feeling that he "ought to learn the openings." He thinks of "the openings" as a systematically arranged body of knowledge, like the Code of Justinian or the Periodic Table of the elements . . .
>
> It is "the opening" that interests us. When the master plays his opening moves, he selects them on the basis of some plan he has in mind. Where this prior consideration is [absent] . . . *he soon evolves a plan from the unforeseen moves he is making.* The play which is to take place in the middle game already exists in embryo in the opening.[4]

A good strategy gives you an image of your venture or goal. Reflexively, you'll look ahead, then back, then sideways to establish "narratives of time and space."[5] In other words, as Chapter 7 elaborates, you must think like an artist, not a bureaucrat: Picture your way into your unknown, play with ideas, symbols, and the practical necessities of your medium, whatever it may be.

Maybe you're a woman who prefers a more intuitive—rather than an engineer's—approach to strategy. Know this: Your mind has no gender. This doesn't mean you lack a problem-solving pattern that works particularly well for *you*. Just don't be fooled into believing that *because you're a woman* your intuitive faculties *must* dominate. I know women (not engineers either) who favor linear, logical analysis and men (not necessarily artists) whose intuitive powers amount to genius. The point is to *integrate* our mental faculties, to come at things with as full a complement of intelligences as possible: spiritual, sensory, musical, visual, relational, kinesthetic comprehension, and more. All these dimensions provide data for minds that are aware.

Shanalei (whose figuring-out skills were discussed in Chapter Four) enjoys concentrating. This forms part of *her* best thinking. Yet Shanalei also "thinks" through her senses. She integrates her rational *and* her intuitive modes of thought. In other words, Shanalei applies as much of herself to a strategy as possible:

Once I'm committed to a task, I'm fully "there"—extremely focused. I have good mental energy. This is power. So I forward my goals by looking through the eyes of whatever I'm doing. If I were waiting on tables, I'd give that my single-minded attention—I'd try to see my actions from the customer's viewpoint.

Strategy for me also includes writing down my goals. I ask myself, "What do I want out of life? What do I know I can do?" Then I wrap deadlines—a time frame—around my dreams by pondering, "If I could do one thing this year to advance my goals, what's most important? Next year?" This then becomes my map—I use it to project my budget or sales goals, "see" the steps I need to take.

Before Neil Simon writes a play, mentally he scans a chronology of at least four major scenes. *Unless* he "sees" these, he shelves the project. His practiced batting eye plots out the work along a clearly sequenced, dramatic line *before* beginning.[6] It was said of Arthur Dake, a master chess player from Portland, Oregon, that "when he sits down at a board and analyzes, he can see fifteen or sixteen moves ahead . . . in an instantaneous glance."[7]

That larger-than-life football coach Vince Lombardi equipped both himself *and* his players with a visible strategy. He combined tangible diagrams with verbal descriptions of his strategies to help others picture his campaign. According to Bart Starr:

The heart of his system was preparation. For nine seasons I watched him . . . diagram his favorite play, the sweep, and talk about it, and I never once got tired of his performance. Every single time I was captivated.

He would go over every assignment, showing exactly how each man fit into the play. He would explain how the flanker, whose main assignment was to get the safety, should first try to bump the halfback, to get him off stride . . . just bursting with enthusiasm . . . he'd show all the different paths the sweep could follow . . . he'd say, "We must make it go. We will make it go. We will run it again and again and again, and we will make it go."[8]

However you cut it, whatever words or metaphors you use, whether in art, sports, business or chess, strategy involves *tactical inner sight*. You "see" not just externals—known or rational possibilities—but also abstract unknowns related to your values, finances, competitors' strengths, or marketplace and technological trends.

Zen masters express this insight in spiritual terms. To hit *any* target we need to "see with other eyes and measure with other measures," and this means entering the deepest spirit of our art.[9] Without discussing spirituality, our inmost stillness, our transcendent mind, I can't address the mind's upper chambers—and this includes gifted, entrepreneurial functioning. Even Horowitz and Reinfeld, when writing of effectiveness in chess, propose that the *inept* display their "spiritual laziness" by failing to defend their territory properly. As fear subsides, spiritual initiative and tactical intelligence increase.

Strategy forces preparation. You study your marketplace of choice *before* plunking down your precious savings for office space or signing contracts with suppliers. If you've ever successfully planned a large party, a conference, or a lengthy vacation, you've tackled this assignment. Prior to hiring caterers or buying airline tickets, you held in mind an overall idea of your objectives. You thought about the weather, your budget, your menu, your guests or friends. *Then* you negotiated your agreements. That's strategy.

One commandment supports the strategic perspective: *Demystify everything.*

## Demystify Strategy

Describe what you want as if to a *very* young child with a fleeting attention span. Play with this process. Forgive yourself (in advance) for the snail's pace of developing your hazy inner pictures or the particulars of your goal. The word *venture* comes from *adventure.* Creating work is, as one retired person put it, an escapade of surprises, not a guided tour. Prepare for numerous detours and perhaps hair-raising side trips.

Merchant-banker Charles Williams likens strategy to "design-ing a giant, interlocking jigsaw puzzle."[10] What do the pieces of *your* occupational puzzle look like? What long-range expenditures do you anticipate? What are your short-range revenue sources? How do your values relate to what you'll do or to those of your customers? What tangible rewards or benefits are you offering? Who precisely are your customers? How might you reach them? This reflection is part "inward listening" and part research. I cannot stress strongly enough its importance or gradualness. Take your time. Indeed, with reflection of this sort: Slower often means faster.

Before starting my human resource firm, I had strategy, vision, and desire—a single-minded, intrinsic notion that I could help gifted, self-actualizing adults function optimally and thereby develop leadership skill. *But,* although I was intensely motivated, I hadn't a clue *how* to do this (and I certainly didn't learn my *hows* in school.* I've never yet written proper business or marketing

---

*Strategy transcends a mere business plan, which spells out how and when you'll do things, like purchase equipment or establish funds. When you're ready to write a business plan, *selected* college courses, competent business consultants, and business books seem wonderfully useful.

plans. However, I am strategically inclined. This is why I insist that strategy and operational planning are *different* and why I admire practical achievement born of this intuitive, conceptual "horse sense" at least as much, if not more, than mere academic training.

Furthermore, my *lack* of formal business training makes me suspect that almost anyone can learn how to plan within the given framework and parameters of *their* vocation. In other words, Woody's inborn carpentry talents uniquely qualify him to strategize about a construction business. Shanalei's talents furnish her with the very insights needed to build her gift-basket enterprise.

Work that feels like the perfect friendship (or that fits us like comfortable shoes) is the key we need to unlock our *particular* humanity. Such work seems to carry with it corresponding data, in the form of insight, intuitions, a given perspective, knowledge, related values, or intelligence. These specifically help us be and do the thing we were meant to do.

Fernando Mateo created his company when he was seventeen, after an employer humiliated him publicly. Mateo told himself, "It's just better that I leave." He got a loan from his father and opened the first Carpet Fashion store, even though academically he was not trained to start a business:

> I didn't know much about anything. And I thought that you buy a product for $10, you sell it for $20, that's the end of it. Fortunately, I had brothers . . . in business, and they told me about insurance and liability and FICA and all of those other things.[11]

I'd guess Mateo's distinctive gifts drove *his* personal vision and that these same talents gave him the strategic sight and faith to become a particular type of contributor within the sphere of his life with others. What we dream of being; what we value; what we long to be, do, and have over the entirety of our life provokes that special spark of genius we each need to "see with other eyes and measure with other measures."

# Demystify Planning

Eventually, our strategies ask us to think about where we'll find supportive, affordable resources for our objectives. Here's where business planning—the other side of the strategy coin—helps. But as author and business consultant Roger Fritz suggests, plans are worthless if we never convert them into *action*.[12] Fritz lists several basic functions—e.g., bookkeeping, banking, insurance—we need to address before we have a viable business. For me, these bits and pieces fell into place as the need for them arose. Had I known enough to follow a planning textbook *before* starting my business and *before* committing myself to my goal, I might have felt overwhelmed by pesky details. Meticulous forecasting interrupts my strategic thinking, especially if I put the cart (i.e., details) before the horse (i.e., vision). I like the motto furnished in the film *Field of Dreams:* "If you build it, they will come."

For me (and this *may* be an individual matter) an inspired strategy creates my operational game plan. I don't sweat the small stuff. As I say, all this seems a very personal preference. Perhaps my approach represents an artist's slant while yours might be more like an engineer's or a brain surgeon's.

A business plan is your detailed, targeted plan of *how* you'll activate your strategic vision. Rodger Touchie's *Self-Counsel* talks to you about such basics: How will you pay for your desk, phones, or payroll? How do you define your market? Your business plan establishes clear identity or a mission statement. Financial, marketing, and start-up (or team) directions are all included in your business plan. Your business plan tells you: "Move there. Wait here. Do this task by *X* date. This CPA or office suite or letterhead or computer or marketing consultant offers the advantage your strategy requires." Such specific, anticipatory questions can well sharpen your professional batting eye.[13]

Several years before I left my tenured public-sector position, I put myself on a strict budget and started saving and investing money. As months turned into years, with long-term purposes in view, I used this time to gain human-resource expertise.

This was a delightful, solitary period—I planned informally, mentally wandered here and there, imagined freely. All that ambiguity added up to heady exhilaration: I must have craved the thrill of not knowing exactly what to do and the inherent self-testing that involved. Although then I couldn't quite articulate what I was doing (or why), I was formulating a campaign for a vocation wholly unique to me. I'd guess this is what every entrepreneur ultimately is doing in some fashion. The more our talents, values, and bid for healthy autonomy influence our career choices, the likelier it is that we'll develop vocational maturity, or the spiritual side of work, along with entrepreneurial prowess.

Leadership theorist Warren Bennis suggests creative leaders look ahead, learn from the past, and turn their whole vision toward the wider context of present realities. All ideas and previous goals get altered as events change: "If there is a spark of genius in the [leader] at all, it must lie in this transcending ability, a kind of magic, to assemble—out of all the variety of images, signals, forecasts, and alternatives—a clearly articulated vision of the future that is at once simple, easily understood, clearly desirable, and energizing."[14]

Foresight, hindsight, depth, and peripheral perception are different aspects of one function: the artist's transcendent mind. We all possess this mind, if only in latent terms. It sparks our genius. Whether "in the leadership function," in the kitchen, or the classroom, this mind is inherently *human,* and as such relates more to our humanity and our deepest consciousness than to any academic or corporate standing. Many so-called primitive or indigenous people possess it. Too many corporate heads do not. Somewhere within ourselves we know that children, homemakers, craftspersons, homeless persons, retired people, and blue- and white-collar workers of all sorts possess a spark of genius *if* they cultivate and use their minds' depths—their healthiest creative intelligence. This is the spark we need to be entrepreneurs, create a business, and ultimately fulfill our vocational promise.

When my first- and second-grade students possessed high self-esteem, *or* (lacking that) when they were gifted along any particular line, *or* (lacking that) even when they were only situationally engrossed in some pleasurable, liberating activity (e.g., like gardening, painting, singing, listening to an engaging story), they exhibited their "spark of genius." *This intelligence was their normal state* and it brought self-confidence, certainty, and trust in their own perceptions.

With this spark, they explored the new and untried. They were discerning. They saw ahead with "other eyes and measures." They somehow absorbed complex questions, danced with these, and made them theirs. Usually, in short order, they finessed their way to answers, achieving insight without teacher interference.

Every aspiring entrepreneur and business leader ought to read well-known educator (and entrepreneur) Dr. Maria Montessori's description of an *average* child's spontaneous victory over a problem:

> [The boy] who was little more than two years old and not at all intelligent in appearance, [was standing] perplexed because he could not remember whether the fork should be set at the right hand or the left. He remained alone while meditating and evidently using all the powers of his mind. The other children older than he watched him with admiration, marveling, like ourselves at the *life developing under our eyes.*\*[15]

Montessori reminds us that we influence thinking (and I must add creative achievement) "merely in a hint, a touch—enough to give a start."[16] Your answers need no force. As you make a gentle, steadfast, and faithful investment in your own spark of genius, you'll reclaim your ability to think for yourself.

Creative people evoke their best plans variously, through playful means as well as all the standard ones. They often envision the land they want to enter before actually setting out. Elsewhere I've outlined my favorite way of clarifying new directions:

---

\*Author's italics for emphasis.

First I draw my "scaffolding" using a private, quite incomprehensible written language of arrows, phrases, line drawings and, sometimes, numbers. (Some of these drawings are over a decade old—I keep adding to them, because even when my notes are indecipherable, I know something is happening, underground.) On the surface, I can't easily trace my overall long-term creative process, so my scribbles are an invaluable personal shorthand. These let me communicate with my nonconscious and, apparently, enable translation of invisible, inexpressible concepts into visible forms and products . . . Notebooks, working blueprints, or drawings and personal papers are all appropriate systems, as are letters and photographs. Each individual has . . . favorite codes.[17]

Woody utilizes a completely different planning code. Computer spread sheets let him envision his next moves. For example, every night he spent five minutes pouring over financial figures to "see" where he could cut costs or manage better:

We had an incredible amount to do before our relocation. We had to fix up and sell our home. I took a shop class to learn how to make fine furniture. It was then, in that early course work, that I had access to really good tools.

Without knowing exactly what I was doing, or how much I was learning, gradually I realized, "Oh, I can do this." In fact, I'd been doing construction work since I was twelve and built my first tree house. A standard joke around our home was that if I couldn't make it as an engineer, I could always build houses.

An auto mechanic I'll call Bob said he rarely plans. Sounding much like Napoleon who said, "Unhappy the general who comes on the field of battle with a system," Bob admits he is impulsive. To me, he is a gifted improviser, inherently tactical. Now sixty-something, he's always been his own boss. When Bob approached retirement, he and his wife moved to an area they loved. Then he spotted rich unexpected opportunities in the new location and made an offer on a service station:

> I didn't plan this. I intended to retire. But I can size up a shop by just looking it over and scanning the books. This one looked good. Keep in mind, I've been in this business for almost forty years. Sure, I mull things over, but most details that other people look at, I leave alone. I'll deal with whatever comes up.
>
> Hell, don't go into business if you can't roll with the ups and downs. Making mistakes is nothing. No matter how much you plan, or think you know, you'll get surprises and then you'd better react properly. This community is cliquish when it comes to a new guy. No planning could have shown me how tightly suppliers and customers can shut you out if they want to. Once I saw that, I adjusted. I have no choice—I have to make it work. You know, "Necessity is the mother of invention." I've never worked for anyone else, and I don't intend to. No textbook taught me how to figure out what's needed. You just have to use your head. That's the fun of it.

# Demystify Marketing

If you lack a feel for (or experience in) marketing, then before attempting to create your own work, study the subject or hire a reputable specialist to guide you. Your decision to study whatever you don't understand becomes part of your strategy—your defensive hedge against your own flaws or ignorance. How will you promote yourself? How will you make your ideas, services, or products known? Who'll want what you can offer? How will you package, administer, or distribute your offerings? These questions call for shrewd analysis of the territory you want to conquer. If you're a word processor, massage therapist, or widget maker, how will others know you're on the planet, ready to make your contribution to them? Find your own terms. Define success for yourself. But rest assured that business security rests on being positively noticed and your particular talents appreciated.

As authors George Dudley and Shannon Goodson suggest, even seemingly hard-nosed salespeople are often terrified of the vulnerability rejection invites:

> The fear of self-promotion is the general condition behind call reluctance in salespeople. It is found in motivated goal-striving people everywhere who have great emotional difficulty promoting themselves. Not limited to salespeople alone, it keeps competent and deserving people in almost every walk of life from being recognized for their contributions and, therefore, from getting ahead.
>
> Too modest to "toot his own horn," a loyal and deserving administrator is not promoted to the next higher position because someone less competent, but more visible, gets the job.[18]

One executive wanted to start his own firm but complained that, although he loves his work, industry competition makes it "impossible to earn a living." It turns out that he detests the selling and marketing functions of his business. He's ashamed or embarrassed to convince potential buyers about the merits of his product. His lack of prosperity attests to the Chinese proverb, "A man without a smiling face must not open a shop."

# Demystify Positioning

I know an astute, well-read man who aspires to the prestigious position of senior vice-president of human resources. He is self-taught and lacks the necessary corporate and peer support for his ambition. Although many self-taught people *do* gain the requisite credibility for the promotions they desire, this individual bridles at the thought of asserting himself as a leader. He said, "People will simply know I'm deserving—it's obvious how much I know. And I hate it when you use that term 'positioning.' I can't imagine crassly positioning myself for any job!"

Positioning involves sophisticated, overtly strategic communications. Marketing and sales activities do not automatically turn us into back-slapping, deceptive fast talkers. This is an old-fashioned idea perpetuated by those who still think all salespeople employ the soiled maneuvers of the unscrupulous. However, sales and marketing *do* require us to situate ourselves (or our products or company) in others' minds so that we can honestly and actively communicate our objectives to them.

Wally Amos founded Famous Amos cookies when his personnel management business hit hard times. He was "grossly undercapitalized" and forced to promote his cookies in outrageous theatrical ways. Once he "traded a day's worth of cookies ($750) for [radio advertising time]." Another time, to capture his consumer's attention, Amos hired professional models to distribute cookies to passersby in Beverly Hills and Hollywood. "I knew I had the best product. All I needed . . . was to convince the public [of it]. In 1975, a star was born and I was its showman."[19]

Without his willingness to conceive of what he wanted and then openly reach for it, without helpful self-beliefs and commitment to his products, Amos would have sorely limited his options. So it is for us. Without positioning skill, we're left to trust "luck" or covert manipulative skills. Or perhaps we sit around passively, hoping that people who have what we want will grant us favors. When a wealthy potential donor expressed dismay at Lady Churchill's emboldened fund-raising tactics, she responded "You have something I want. How am I supposed to get it if I don't ask?"

You need others to help you succeed. This doesn't mean exploiting anyone but simply exchanging something of your's—

ideas, time, energy, talent—for something they have. The people you need *most* probably lead busy lives. They face, as you may, nearly chaotic levels of pressure and uncertainty. Help them *hear* your message. When you discuss your services, products, or vision with potential clients (or your manager, family, and friends), consider who they are and how little time they have to listen. Figure out how you'll get (and keep) their ear. Just tell them, in uncluttered, *diplomatic* terms, what you want and what you're prepared to offer them in exchange. Advertising executives Al Ries and Jack Trout advise brevity and a clear focus: "in communication, as in architecture, less is more. You have to sharpen your message to cut into the mind. You have to jettison the ambiguities, simplify the message and then simplify it some more if you want to make a long-lasting impression."[20]

Find or create an opening in the other's mind for your message. You're trying to capture someone's attention. Are you afraid of potential rejection by your customers? Do you think you'll demean yourself by being frank? Do you resent selling or believe at heart you're an impostor? Do your own ambitions threaten you? If at some level you fear either failure *or* success, then for heaven's sake, keep your day job while, strategically, you plan ways around this.

To turn vision into a strategic plan, assess yourself:

- *How, specifically, am I studying the* marketplace *of my venture?*

- *How am I researching specific ways to add value to my customer or client?*

- *How might I demystify my planning tasks? Who could help me untangle the knots of technical complexity in my endeavor?*

- *Practically speaking, what am I doing to utilize my* own *spark of genius?*

- *How might I position my product or service in the niche I hope to enter?*

Although devising a strategy is subtle, it's not complicated. The next time you notice your teenager waiting for precisely the right moment to borrow your car keys, you'll see a fine example of strategy at work.

## A SUMMARY STRATEGY

Once upon a time, a fabulously wealthy king had a son whom he adored. The boy was bright and handsome—perfect in every way—except one: He had a severely hunched back. This saddened the king no end. So he proclaimed that a huge reward would go to the person who figured out how to heal the boy's back. Months and months passed without a solution. Wise men and women with good ideas traveled to the palace from all over the region. But no one knew what to do.

Then one day, a famous guru happened into the kingdom and heard about the problem. "I don't want your reward," said the tiny woman (who was herself all scrunched over with age and wrinkled up like a prune). "But," she added, "I do have your answer." This was her advice:

In the center of your courtyard, you must construct a sculpture—an exact replica of your dear son, with one exception: Its back must be straight and lovely in appearance. That's all. Trust God for the healing.

With that, the Master disappeared and the king's artisans set to work. In no time, a beautiful marble sculpture sat in the center of the courtyard. Every day as the little boy played, he studied the figure admiringly. He started to feel, "Why that's me! That looks exactly like me." Every day, the prince gazed lovingly at the sculpture until he identified with it.

Bit by bit, the boy's back straightened. One day, a year or so later, as the king watched his son frolicking in the gardens, he suddenly noticed the prince's back was totally healed. The young boy's identification with the marble sculpture had been so complete that he believed it represented him—straight back and all. Body obeyed belief.[21]

*Try This:*

- For a week or more, keep a journal of observational notes about people you admire who are already being and doing what you'd like to be and do. Make sure you're watching individuals you respect. Be selective. Choose the best of the best. You need not know the persons (or be around them physically) to study and identify with them.
- Stop waiting for "mentors" to discover you. Use *your* imagination. Watch television (e.g., news shows, interviews, documentaries) or movies that display the life moves and mind of those whose talents, accomplishments, or vocation you would like to emulate (not imitate).
- After a month or two, review your notes, reflecting on the patterns of your choices:
  How do you *feel* about your selections? Are you excited about your choices and the possibilities you now conceive of for yourself? Are you disheartened? Does it seem like your selections have qualities you can't imagine developing?

(If your own observations—and your mental discussion—depress you, visit a competent counselor. Feelings are superb messengers from the unconscious. You can make significant progress by discussing painful or unpleasant emotions with someone who has studied what psychiatrist David Viscott calls "the language of feelings."[22]

· What victories, obstacles, or attributes do you routinely admire? (One person may primarily admire Olympic athletes; another, business leaders; a third, "ordinary people.")

· How do you interpret your observations? What are the vocational implications of your predictable choices?

Think of this exercise as a way to use your "inner camera." Throughout life, what pictures have you collected for your mental scrapbook? How might your selections further or undermine your belief in your ability to think strategically?

Like the little prince who changed, *bit by bit*, because of his identifications and self-beliefs, your self-beliefs get influenced by the mental company you keep.

# CHAPTER 7

# High Spiritual Intelligence

*Discovering—and creating—vocation requires
discernment. We must learn how to increase
distinctiveness under varying circumstances, serve
our interests as well as those of others. Searching
for answers, over time, we integrate daily
activities with larger, more profound realities.
Our "how to do this?" inquiry, when serious and
steadfast, draws forth spiritual intelligence
wherein we learn what's right for us and
surrender to that truth.*

Leonardo da Vinci believed every sculptor should construct a figure so that its pose reveals its soul. I propose the entirety of our life's endeavors reveals *our* soul. Becoming faithful to our gifts and inclinations, hearing the call or press within to be whole, we find vocation—that line of activity we intention-ally use to grow as a person. This growth builds our life. Our work permits or forces emotional and intellectual capability, the cultivation of true competence and an integrity: completion, fullness of being. Whatever one does, whether as day laborer or diplomat, when one conceptualizes work in this way it becomes vocation.

In this sense, we are never "out of work." Now our job is to unfold, to reveal, our true nature within the context of service to ourselves and our community. Now, continually, we transcend our old mind, renew it, cast off its vain imaginings and outdated perspectives.

Discovering—and creating—vocation requires discernment. We'll need to know how we might increase our distinctiveness under various circumstances. We'll want to serve our own needs and interests as well as those of others. If we are searching for answers, over time we find ourselves integrating our daily activities—the little things we do and say—with larger, more profound realities. We regain lost capacities (as some would say complete the Gestalt of our life) by coming at things from a unified perspective. And now we *use* tasks, our ordinary labors to fulfill our destiny. Many single parents say, "Even if I must take on three jobs, I'm going to support my child properly."

For them, parenting *is* vocation. Their three or four jobs, however menial or grand, are merely tasks to use at varying crossroads of life to get the job done, make their contribution to the world, *be* responsible, loving caregivers. Each one who fulfills his or her vocation becomes a vital cell in the body of humankind. Additionally, whether we are parents or plumbers, vocation becomes our organic movement of self, seeking wholeness. "Making money" per se is incidental. True vocation is never about money—although money somehow follows. And in various amounts. In this I sense positive emotions and energy (e.g., love, faith, fascination, fulfillment, challenge, etc.) attracts income.

Shanalei reminds those who would create their work to consider the spiritual dimension of enterprise:

> Be sure you head toward what you love. Commit to your goal for the long haul. One reason people don't last is that they don't stick through the tough times. They idealize their dreams, they don't prepare for the "dog work"—the unappealing details like filling out credit forms, marketing, even sweeping up the office.
>
> When love drives your ambitions, good things flow toward

you. Love—and not the romantic type, either—is pure power. It's energizing. Having all those customers or colleagues support my dreams is, for me, an incredible high. Of course there are plenty of low times, but just being alive is a joy. It's the joy, the love, that uplifts me.

We know vocation beckons us when our values, talents, or longings move us, or when we willingly persist, despite hardships. Author Logan Pearsall once wrote that when we love the drudgery involved in our work, *that's* vocation. All creaturely definitions of "success," all human systems for garnering security essentially mislead us. The main point is to work from a perspective and stance that lets us become ourselves and thereby complete ourselves uniquely.

One person may earn $250,000 a year; another might save $100,000 (over the course of their career) to live off the interest; a third could make a minimum hourly wage at some temporary job. Whoever hits the mark of their own vocation "succeeds"—does with life what they feel *born* to do. Both Get-Rich philosophies *and* frugality programs seem to miss the goal of helping us find true fulfillment. No matter how full or empty our coffers, *subjectively* we're always rich when we are true to our vocation and "poor"—joyless, frustrated, victimized, defeated—when we betray it.

Contrast the befuddlement of people who don't know what they want from life to the clarity of those in advanced states of vocational awareness. For the latter, work is like play. They say, *"I'd pay to do this,"* or *"I can't believe I'm making money at this!"* Our work is like prayer. This is so whether people are "religious" or not. When we're at one with our work, routine chores invite experience of our soul's pure animating essence. This is spiritual. We forget ourselves. Worries and preoccupations leave us. We feel dedicated to something beyond ourselves. We aim high. We sense, "I *am* a teacher (or an engineer or parent). *Not,* "I wish I could be one."

# Vocational Integration[1]

Our own low perspective keeps us low, slavishly tied to circumstances and needing reassurance, direction, external motivations or incentives. We are either indecisive or driven by fear and greed or we want our achievements to transpire as if by magic. Our best life comes as we accept leadership—and it is spiritual largely—over what we're doing, as we think about our undertakings in terms of what we value.

Even though conditions may require us to continue doing "inauthentic" jobs, like the single mother quoted above, our reasons for taking on such work are our own. One woman who always wanted to be a singer found she had too many fears and insecurities to enter that field. She had talent but lacked ego strength. Every audition was a torture. Actualizing vocation (in her case, some sort of musical expression) involves addressing fear, becoming *fit* enough to do that which we sense we're meant to do.

Our own development transforms daily labors into mature vocation and thereby sanctifies our activities. The theologian Martin Buber's thought—that when we love we "penetrate" existence with our "active love"—applies to vocation: becoming self-aware, we grow more capable of loving. Part of this is synonymous with loving ourselves properly. This ongoing exertion, this practical way of relating to ourselves (and eventually to others) is *spiritual.*

To build a life we desire means, ultimately, we'll "walk our talk"; we'll demonstrate our high ideals and standards, whether in the kitchen or the boardroom. Capabilities and effective execution of our plans are required, not merely transcendent, etherial discussions with supportive confidantes and counselors. Spirituality is, in everyday terms, often grubby. Whatever else it is, it's also *real.*

Creating work we love asks us to choose truthfully, to *do* whatever brings us closer to self-realization. At one moment we'll control our temper. At the next we'll be explicitly forthright—

perhaps downright rude. We'll pay our bills on time or get up two hours early to write the article that we suspect will launch our career. None of this is automatic. Such behaviors often go against the grain of our comfort-loving natures, which is why some entrepreneurs (primarily people who move beyond survival work to create their vocation) seem heroic to me. And spiritual.

One man whose family told him his achievement drives were off base (and therefore unworthy) learned to legitimize his desire to continue. "Each time I step out of my comfort zone, I'm invigorated. But then, immediately, I'm like a deer frozen in fright by oncoming headlights. It takes my all to claim the life I want."

This claim is our bid for wholeness. We may experience an anxious search for truth.[2] Perhaps now we take sabbaticals from work, marriage, or parenthood to scout about for authentic answers. Or, feeling our corporate career is pointless, we may obsess about how to put meaning back into our lives.

Not everyone who starts a business or creates work is "in love" with their work. Not everyone is emotionally *ready* for love. Think of the refugee who runs a corner fruit stand to survive. Although we can create work almost wherever we are emotionally,* when we're reliably ourselves, we *learn* to express our loves, and not feign loyalty to pointless interests or hurtful, potentially exploitative people. We don't pretend to love retailing while, deep down, we're pining away to be landscapers. I've known young corporate executives who, as excited new parents, buried their enthusiasms lest their management think they'd lost their aggressive, competitive edge. In a similar vein, writers say that if they do three "pot-

---

*Sometimes people with serious mental health problems ask "how" to create work they love. As I am explaining: spiritual intelligence, lucidity, and a strategically inventive awareness are only some characteristics of the "inner entrepreneur." Psychiatrist William Glasser has repeatedly written the main task—for *all* of us—is to get as strong (i.e., mentally healthy) as we can, in order to gain endurance, staying power and the fighting, self-renewing spirit for the life we want. When you think about it, what's the alternative?

boilers" (i.e., three projects created primarily for money or prestige), their talent will evaporate. It takes time, practice, and deep desire to live an authentic life.

When I was a tenured public school administrator, I took a year's leave without pay to sort out my future. I wasn't ready to start my own practice. I told my management that I was returning to graduate school. This was true. In my organization, this was also *the only* acceptable reason to request a leave. I did *not* say I needed a break from constant pressure, nor did I mention I intended to live in the country and write books. This was my private agenda. I kept it to myself. I wondered excitedly, *"Is this possible for me? Can I do that? Do I dare?"* My creative output soared as I stepped toward my truths—but I did all this gradually, as I experienced myself ready.

An acquaintance calls this reshuffling phenomenon "raising the ante" of experience. Whenever her ambitions shift upwards so that she craves an enhanced *quality* of life, she says she must "notch up" or elevate her behavior—give up security-based or counterproductive habits. A woman I'll call Esther notched up her activities at a time many people cash in the chips of their careers.

# Esther's Story

When she was in her sixties (and just widowed), Esther began studying for a ministerial degree. Esther felt she'd have a long, healthy life and wanted to live "as a whole person, not merely someone who held the title of 'minister.'" More recently, at her eightieth birthday celebration, Esther was surrounded by her grown children and hundreds of friends to whom she has ministered over the years through lectures, private counseling, and church-related programs. To Esther, building a life involves progressively increasing her spiritual awareness:

Back in 1950, when my husband was still alive, I searched for something to do with my life. I then worked in a drugstore and was very shy. I'd go to church, sit in the back row and would slip out at the end of the services so as not to disturb anyone.

I worried how I'd make it financially. We'd never saved money, and I didn't know what I'd do. I began leaning on my faith, since that's all I had. Then I found a job managing the apartment we'd lived in. Also I kept working at the drug store. I loved that work.

Gradually I saved money and invested it. I now said to myself, "I'm going to keep moving ahead—no matter what." I told myself that living is a lifetime job and that it takes wisdom to receive what I call "divine guidance." We need this to become discerning and effective. I wanted that wisdom in an intense way and gave myself over completely to working for it.

Like Esther, the vocationally integrated tend to be emotionally grounded. They function reliably despite loss or disappointment. They continually reinvent themselves, establish healthy relationships and connect to others openly, cooperatively. Maslow termed such behaviors *"real satisfiers."* Appreciating this, we see why vocation feeds our natural hunger for friendships (and nourishes community life), and why survival work (wherein we labor single-mindedly for money or for other ultracompetitive or fear-based goals) may cripple relationships and demean the integrity of life as a whole. For instance, Esther satisfies her life's genuine purposes by "helping others help themselves, teaching people how to think so that they can be their best." She says, "You know, we do direct our own thinking. After all is said and done we are responsible for our lives. Each one of us must have a purpose in life in order to be happy."

Whatever the outward appearance, to the vocationally integrated work becomes *service to self and others.* We must not judge anyone about this. Some people—be they artists, philosophers, or financial planners—need to work in solitude, yet serve through contribution. Vocational integration involves the *spirit,* not the form, of work. Nikos Kazantzakis's line, "I said to the almond tree, 'Sister, speak to me of God,' And the almond tree blossomed," describes the mutually sustaining, dynamic nature of this. Esther's progress *as a person* serves others, is somehow spiritual in its rightness and fit—and is comprised of an *evolving* consciousness. *As she blossoms, she serves the greater good.*

Having a vocation in no way implies we reject corporate positions or that we must work alone. Far from it. Some of our greatest leaders can only fulfill their vocational needs through corporate or political organizations. Being ourselves, we'll find much to do along *any* given line of endeavor (like carpentry, nursing, accounting, parenting, policing, and so on). The more vocationally integrated we become, the more we enjoy our "doing"—intend to be and do a thing and gain a fuller dimension of ourselves. Rather than splitting ourselves up into little, fictitious bits, when expressing our vocation we realize there is *always* something more to be, more to do, some remunerative work to take on (if only through a barter or volunteer system). We ourselves *are* the work—the integrity of being, or "workmanship," that transmits skill, value, or enthusiasms to others. Integrity like this is always spiritual.

One man who was fired from his sales job considered finding another similar post. During a career counseling session, he realized he had never liked sales. Being athletic, he started cleaning houses temporarily, just to make ends meet. Moving about, using his body appealed to him. His own enjoyments led him further along. Today he owns a house-cleaning establishment. This brief illustration shows how many people "build a life" merely by addressing their authentic purposes.

A friend's real estate firm experienced a financial slump. For years, as a side interest, he'd studied massage therapy and loved that. With free time on his hands, now he intensified these studies. Soon he began a massage-therapy practice. He currently works part-time in both occupations. Most of his massage clients are stressed-out real estate agents, worried about low sales.

It is painful to be fired and start anew. It can be scary to accept the cold harsh fact that work which once gave us pleasure no longer remunerates us—that *we* must change. This is where our ability to reinvent ourselves pays off. *If* we function from the vantage point of our healthy inner summonings—intuition, a sudden impulse to tackle something new—we're employing *spiritual* intelligence to get answers, to extinguish erroneous beliefs or evolve out of seemingly dead-end circumstances.

Our deepend awareness shows us when it's time to change and how to respond adroitly. The Zen Buddhists say that when we see reality as one seamless, unitive whole, all sorts of "extraordinary possibilities come to us without our seeking them."[3] Heightened consciousness structures strategic sight, mysterious power, what Esther terms "divine guidance." As we cultivate the synergy of our own inner forces—for instance, abstracting or conceptualizing skills—our spiritual intelligence increases.

Taking time to *be* makes us brighter. Walks in nature, yoga, or meditation, listening to music are pastimes that shift our sights. Although it's only human to feel impatient to earn profits or gain directional clarity, it's also symptomatic of an undeveloped psyche. Children want to get There quickly. A Tibetan proverb says the faster we try to go, the slower our progress. In many matters, the less we rush, the better. Relaxing into who and what we are is healing. Simple *being* raises spiritual intelligence. John Muir's thought, "So-called sentimental, transcendental dreaming seems the only sensible and substantial business that one can engage in,"[4] suggests *how* we might proceed.

Generally, we do not *leap* from a survival mentality into supernatural, inventive wisdom. Even Saul (who became Paul when graced by God, "as a light from heaven flashed . . . and he fell to the ground and heard God's voice,"[5]) underwent a lengthy seasoning, during which his faith and leadership ripened. If we've led an inept or counterfeit existence, it is unlikely that one self-help book or quick-fix weekend will permanently enlighten us.

Neither can we foresee our "career path" in advance. Who could have predicted where Esther's growth would ultimately lead? Esther's professional effectiveness depends on spontaneity, on her finding, then expressing, the sacred images that energize her life.

This is exactly what artists require. And entrepreneurs. One man laughed at the notion of finding a "magic formula" for starting a company:

> *You build a business by studying your field. Proceed cautiously and professionally—don't just run to quickie seminars that hand you a notebook of "to-do" lists (like those real-estate weekends costing hundreds of dollars, offered primarily when the market is depressed).*

No parent, teacher, or mentor can tell us *precisely how* to create fulfilling work because vocational gold and "real satisfiers" are buried far beneath conventional, trivialized responses—hidden within our inmost states. Today, even secular educators remind adult learners to lean on helpmates like prayer or art and music therapies when they require complex, subtly nuanced answers. Vocation comes as you *discover and express your own identity.* This discovery is a process that is both work and art.

# Work As Art

Artists—not just business-school professors—should *teach* entrepreneurial skills. Standard university MBA programs could enrich their offerings by integrating art or jazz improvisation courses into their humdrum, academic fare. Many MBA instructors are uncreative. Only a few have actually created or run a successful venture.

We learn best when we're learning about ourselves, when we're discovering truths that speak of inner *and* outer realities, when we're finding out what makes us unique—and like others—within the community. The discovery of identity calls for authentic guides. As Maslow wrote, they are rare. The details of daily behavior betray everyone's facades:

You may be in the middle of a fight, and your guts are writhing with anger, but if the phone rings, you pick it up and sweetly say hello. Authenticity is the reduction of phoniness toward the zero point.[6]

Almost all gifted artists strive to mesh inner feelings or vision with marketplace realities. Some actually figure out ways to earn money doing what they love. Each does so in slightly idiosyncratic ways.

In this, the most proficient artists court their moods and emotions. They remain hospitable to both inner and outer cues, stay open to diversity and stimulation. The great graphic artist and eloquent teacher Ben Shahn said his best work communicated some *"haunting inner image"* onto externals, "When such an image appears before us in our work . . . by recognition of something almost unknown that we are searching for, such recognition is immediate and there is great joy in it."[7]

To be sure, our creative process is disruptive, but when we're otherwise healthy, it eventually stimulates *self*-appreciation. One executive who worked in an ultracompetitive environment knew he was miserable:

My company has deteriorated over the years. Management is uncaring and totally stressed. It's a matter of time before the senior team expires or faces bankruptcy. We employees are expected to produce faster and faster; quality control is a joke. This strikes me as inhumane and irresponsible. Maybe I'm not enough of a shark to make it here. One option is to leave.

I'm too young to retire. I have energy and good ideas. I want independence. Maybe I'll buy a franchise. I'm amazed at how much lighter I feel just having conceived a desirable goal.

As we complete small, intended projects (even if we fall short of our idealized aims), healthy self-esteem and confidence surge. Still we could have conflicts or feel both joy and regret in moving on. Make no mistake about it: Sacrifices are involved in our uncovering of vocation. Letting go of what was, saying good-bye to old friends, is part of this graduation. We consciously choose these separations because the truths we're reaching for demand it. This too is spiritual.

New ideas (and the ancillary goals these trigger) take up time. A human resource specialist said, *"Unstructured time is an incredibly valuable planning tool."* The more time she takes to daydream, the more she wants. As vocational awareness deepens, you'll no longer mechanically chase money or a cool, conventional career, you'll birth your very *self.* Ben Shahn described this self-unfolding better than anyone, saying that for an artist: *"the self is a content\* . . .* the source of whatever truth [our art] can discover. It is constantly invoked, consulted, conversed with. . . . Whatever the world knows of the self it knows through the arts and not through science."[8]

The common remark, *"I wonder why it took so long for the light to come on,"* suggests, as noted, that *years* may pass before we can logically articulate what's wanted. Waiting for truths to come out of hiding can be frustrating. How does one explain to a spouse or peers why the status quo is being disrupted?

When an executive lost her job, she accepted unemployment for a year (instead of looking for another job), using the year to finish writing a book she'd begun in college. For her, the choice was both agony and blessing:

> Even with the deferral of bills, I've doubted my sanity. My fears and resistances underscore the negative comments from family and friends. Still, this feels life affirming. I'm finally risking for what I've always wanted. If I must take a part-time job to keep on keepin' on, so be it. It's worth it.

Perhaps only actualizing adults find enough personal reward in such risks to accept the turmoil involved (e.g., family/inner conflict, struggle, doubts, etc.). They love some intrinsic piece of

---

*Author's italics for emphasis.

their work or find peak moments in it. If we ask the executive why she willingly embraces an agonizing choice, she'll probably answer, "I just get so much pleasure out of writing."

*Chariots of Fire* illustrates how the motives of the vocationally mature differ from those who work for recognition or traditional "success." Two Olympic runners compete for a gold medal. They are both heroic, honorable—incredibly virtuous. But one, Harold Abrahams, runs to prove his worth ("obsessed with winning . . . forced to battle prejudice in an English society that treated him as an alien"), the other, Eric Liddell, a Scottish missionary, races "for the glory of God."[9] To me, Liddell epitomizes a higher state of vocational awareness. His perceptual level is far different than Abrahams's. Liddell receives spiritual uplift and an almost palpable physical pleasure from running. He also loves missionary work. His vocation is neither about *career nor money;* it's doing God's will. (This also suggests that a vocation's tasks or preoccupations may change over the course of life.) When Liddell's sister chides him for neglecting his church responsibilities, he answers,

> I believe that God made me for a purpose. For [missionary work]. But He also made me fast, and when I run, I feel His pleasure. To give it up would be to hold Him in contempt. . . . To win is to honor Him.[10]

Lest I give the impression that vocational maturity is somehow linked to being religious, let me repeat that it is not. It is, however, distinctly *spiritual*: Being a runner or a missionary (or a bookkeeper or computer programmer) animates our essential nature *when* we're being authentic.

Our vivid emotions speak of this vibrancy, or its lack. These may surface through feelings, dreams, slips-of-the-tongue. When we envy others for what *they* have, our hidden self is talking. We could want to emulate the one we're envying. We may have denied something special within ourselves. At my lectures, audience members often describe distress about some vague unknown. They ascribe anxieties as "fear of the unknown" or voice anger at social injustice. Most want me (or a magazine article or book) to quickly extinguish "negative" feelings, to list easy solutions that magically turn discomfort into right, profitable action. One person from Iowa said with obvious good humor, "I came here to get *the* answer. I thought you'd tell me exactly what to do with my whole life but here you are, saying it takes time to find meaningful answers and that these are within myself." Almost all accomplished artists and actualizing adults try to *amplify* subjective distress, not silence it.

Creative encounter with purposeful activity involves coaxing out and *using* inner chaos, not just delighting in ecstatic moods. Torpor, sadness, restlessness, fear—all these are powerful energies awaiting release through our life's purposes. These energies also contain huge stories of information. Such emotions, rightly expressed, are like fuel. Resourceful, productive people often feel conflicted. When wrestling with adversity or some hidden aspirations, they use every feeling as a resource in their search for truth. Inventiveness is a complex process; it can be uncomfortable. It uses (even explains) emotional turmoil. Creativity expert John Briggs proposes that intangible factors (vision, talent, or background) blend in an integral process, as "a single, fluid gem":[11]

> The pattern of creative lives testify to a creator's absorption in work that is so overwhelming that it comes to direct the creator's whole existence. Picasso one day informed his mistress . . . *Everybody has the same energy potential. The average person wastes it in a dozen little ways. I bring mine to bear in one thing only: my painting, and everything is sacrificed to it—you and everyone else, myself included.*[*][12]

Too many of us distrust anything unfamiliar like deep joy or sadness, or a nightmare or the odd instinct. We want our creativity neat and tidy. We expect "courses" on the subject to be predictable, replete with properly spaced coffee-breaks and take-home outlines for orderly follow-up study. Briggs warns us rightly:

---

*Author's italics for emphasis.

Creativity is an "absorbing flame," and our false assumptions about our creativity "may be rooted in uneasiness, even an aversion . . . to anything that seems truly different."[13]

The famous sculptor Giacometti suffered intense agitation before starting to work. He stalled as long as possible. We stall, too. We may naively expect insights to pop out instantly, like a fast-food drive-through. Whether we're carving a piece of marble or a business plan, our creative process has distinctive rules. Our willingness to accept discomfort (and perhaps a snail's pace of progress) helps overcome blocks.

*Spiritual* intelligence utilizes every delay and experience for its own purpose. It melds our archetypal drives and germinating talents with imagination. Over time, we conceive fresh possibilities for work and, restating Freud's premise, learn to love and labor productively. All this seems to me a grace, a robust validation of psychic health. Gradually, our vocation transforms work, as Robert Frost wrote, into "play for mortal stakes . . . for Heaven and the future's sakes."[14]

# Developing Spiritual Intelligence

Spirituality implies any number of diverse drives to know, enrich, and express our inner life.[15] While religion is our particular, potentially *fixed* system of beliefs (with all its special rites, language, membership, and worldview), spirituality is soft, un-fixed, and potentially embarrassing. After all, how would you describe your "spirit"? What words do you use to speak about the ineffable core of your creative or virtuous self, your mystical feelings, or that subtle sense of sacredness that drives your quest for goodness, for meaning, or sacrifice for family?[16]

Spirituality is an intelligence in its own right. Much like musical ability, which gives us an ear for melodies others may not hear, spiritual acuity lets us love, forgive, or "see" our next steps. Our journey from a fearful life to a bold, loving, and contributive one depends largely on spiritual "talent." This invites our faith. Without connecting to our healthiest, positive inner drives, we cannot even conceive of the extent to which our own talents might fulfill us. Nor can we discern "how" to unfold a vocation within the context of our present circumstances. Esther's spiritual intelligence—not just her linear or rational faculties—revealed far-off goals that seemed, initially, unrealizable. She used "divine guidance" to climb up her vocational ladder.

Even a reasonably high spiritual I.Q. (which, thankfully, no standardized test can measure) brings insight, ability, and an unrelenting wish to make sense of unintelligible cues: love, longings, feelings of gratefulness, our need to serve, or to relinquish the familiar for the unknown and so on. To the spiritually maturing person, these feelings become a new standard for making quality choices that ultimately revise life. The spiritual person embodies critical intellectual capabilities, such as heightened awareness that sees problems as challenges or that blends logic and intuition. One gifted entrepreneur said, "I use daily obstacles as a means to show my talents. This takes me a step closer to *being* all that I am."

# Adopting an Artist's Process

Each spiritual quality listed above is *practical.* Joy, faith, patience, endurance, and the synergy of our higher intellectual faculties are powers. These produce our seen world—sales results, expansion plans, customer relationships. A neighbor in business for herself endured years of financial insecurity while starting up her company. She credits faith, prayer, and her "absolute refusal to worry about money"—all decidedly spiritual choices—for her solvency:

> I have faith that I haven't been brought this far in life to fail. My creative process reveals itself as I go. I don't know "how" it works, but it does.

Last year, a large job ended. It had carried me economically during the past months. I didn't know where I'd make up the revenue when the project was over. I prayed about it. I told myself, "Something right will emerge." Then I let go of all worry. I absolutely refused to worry. I used my down time (when I had little to do) to prepare for things I wanted to do. Within three or four days, two hefty, well-paying projects came along to replace the concluded one.

This is an example of how positive faith lets spiritually maturing people *live* their cherished values. A colleague confided that aesthetics are increasingly important: "I want to add beauty to everything I do. I don't know yet what that means, but I'm retiring early so I can explore several ideas." Similarly, another corporate executive took a sabbatical to create her future: "I want a small, gorgeous space somewhere—a tiny room of my own—in which to counsel and coach people as they grow spiritually. I need a year off to figure out how to manage this."

Such choices are spiritually elevated, even if expressed in secular forms. (Remember Isaiah 30:21: "Thine ears shall hear a word behind thee saying, 'This is the way.'") *Hearing* that you need to express beauty or that you want to encourage others can free you for genuine success. It is primarily self-actualizing adults who take time to listen to their needs. Theirs is a practical (if also potentially costly and inconvenient) goal: to hear, with tactical comprehension, that which is yet *unformed* but already mysteriously seeded and fully alive within.

We comprehend this lively inner stirring when we are spiritually alert. Our watchfulness is perfected with use, trust, and faithful investments in whatever small acts advance our animating essence. Then, with our thoughts, our words, and our choices we build our future.

Imagine the insecurities Esther must have felt before entering ministerial school. She was alone, starting a new enterprise, concerned about finances. Yet she stubbornly determined to keep moving ahead—no matter what:

Our church offered a ministerial program which I wanted to join. I didn't have the prerequisite years of college, and I had many self-doubts. My minister supported my goals, and soon the church gave me equivalency credit. I took the course primarily for my own spiritual growth and knowledge. When it was time for me to write my thesis, I didn't even know what a thesis was. All I had was a burning desire to be a more effective, complete person. So I plugged along with the thesis and was so proud of myself when I completed the course.

It took me several years to get the necessary licensing. I knew that I had capability but felt very uncertain. It was a gradual process for me to overcome my personal limits and erroneous self-beliefs. Eventually, I was invited to join the Board of Directors at my church. Then I was voted its president. All the while, I kept studying and practicing my faith and doing everything I could to grow. I was already in my seventies.

Regardless of chronological age, the vocationally maturing know that no one else can rescue them from the hard choices of authentic living. If *immature,* we may hunt for dominant others to tell us *how* to live. Universally, our most revered teachers and mentors encourage us to find our own way. In like fashion, well-loved myths, fables, fairy tales, and parables (and nearly all enduring films) repeat these spiritual principles: Quiet yourself. Attend to the inner still, small voice. Know thyself. *Be* thyself. Then you'll discover "how" to live.

# Unmasking Ourselves

Another advantage of working without pretense is becoming what psychiatrist Erich Fromm called a "productive type": an individual who *feels* effective, and who senses an inherent potential.

Like Esther, our experience of potential lets us shape our

destiny. We feel valuable or worthy of reaching for what seems rightfully ours—the proper, well-timed expression of talent or means of belonging in the world. I've heard people say that as soon as they *felt* deserving, money, career opportunities, and friendships fell into place. Our own virtues—like courage, tenacity, truthfulness—comprise a substantial *power*. Virtue liberates our wits appropriately, and lets us believe or know we can reach for what we want. Then we develop ourselves in the concreteness of everyday life.

A corporate client had been at the mercy of a manipulative consultant. He began asserting himself by saying what he felt and asking for what he wanted. Within months things fell into place without further tension:

> I've stopped walking on eggs around people who might reject me for saying what I want. I feel increasingly hopeful—like I can solve normal business conflicts. Differences still arise, but somehow I now feel a current of strength inside and that "directs" my speech.

Authentic people project this honest "current of strength" effectively—so that others receive it. We *like* to be around someone who's real or productive. We *want* to associate with those whose sincerity we feel. We eagerly hire people whose upbeat energy or clarity influences *us* for the better. They're reliable. They keep promises. All these traits—reliability, orderliness, zest—are spiritual. Generally, productive people get our repeat business.

To be a creative, functioning person we must be secure enough to unmask ourselves, as Fromm suggests. This means we'll be truth-tellers about our intentions or values. Unmasking is a spiritual assignment that has occupied the minds of great saints and creative giants of every era and all cultures. As a boy, Leo Tolstoy, Russia's (indeed, the world's) creative genius, longed to live authentically. But family influences redirected him toward fame and wealth. Finally in later years verging on suicide, he revived his early passions and expressed his seeking in an un-masked universal voice:

> My question . . . was the simplest [one], lying in the soul of every man from the foolish child to the wisest elder: . . . "What will come of what I am doing to-day or shall do tomorrow?" "What will come of my whole life?" . . .
> It can also be expressed thus: "Is there any meaning in my life that the inevitable death awaiting me does not destroy?"[17]

For fulfillment's sake, in saintlike fashion, eventually we'll *love* our own unmasking. The demands of consciously created work teach perseverance: to function—to face, not run from, obliga-tions. This is truly a hero's job. Sooner or later, we'll meet the uncertainties that grow out of our new work. These are not just economic. We'll have to pit ourselves against fear, hesitation, and self-crippling thoughts. When affluent privileged persons undergo such unmasking, I've seen them arrange matters so that they toss themselves out of overly fixed circumstances. One wealthy execu-tive confided, "I don't know why I'm moving across the country. I simply feel that I must." A homemaker-realtor said, "It would be easier to stay where I am—in this job and setting—but, as Thoreau said when he left Walden, 'This is all the time I have available for this spot.'"

Our struggle to make our life our own humanizes us. Contrary to common belief, it is not easy conditions that provide our most valuable returns, but full, passionate engagement with our truths. This requires self-questioning along these open-ended lines:

- *What has meaning for me?*

- *Are my talents adequate for my truest ambitions?*

- *Can I earn enough from the new enterprise to meet my commitments?*

- *By changing careers am I merely running away from what I fear, loathe, or find tedious? Do I truly feel that, as Thoreau put it, "This is all the available time I have for this endeavor"?*

• *What techniques or support systems can I find to strengthen myself and stay grounded while transitioning into something new?*

In the final analysis, our growth toward high vocational awareness requires positive faith. Faith gets us through those tough, dark times. Even if we have some self-doubts, faith is one of those unseen spiritual "talents" that lets us commit to our ideals. We strengthen faith by trusting it. This doesn't mean denying doubts or facts. We simply move forward as we can, where we are now. There is, as Pastor Fredrick Price cautions, a difference between presumption and faith. Healthy discernment is part of high spiritual intelligence. Until we notice sufficient positive faith (i.e., in ourselves, in others, in God—whatever) to reach for what we want, we're not *ready* to move ahead.

Positive faith—our "I can do this" attitude—stimulates various gifts. Positive faith puts us back in control, sets up promising conditions. The Bible tells us *faith is the substance of desired, unseen things*. Our faith attracts bright prospects, clarifies thinking, rids our mind of cobwebs and ghosts. Faith helps us use our capacities as loyal servants to build a life we value. Friendships, where we reside, how we spend our leisure time or relate to co-workers or neighbors—these building blocks of life come under wholesome rearrangement as positive faith increases.

Sometimes in a crisis we're thrown into the unknown before we've cultivated sufficient faith to consciously approach it. For the able, this is not all bad and may be experienced as a thrilling, if also scary, learning adventure. Nearly one hundred years ago, William James—then America's favorite philosopher and psychologist—asked us to suppose we were mountain climbing and came to an abyss "from which the only escape" was by an awesome leap. James concludes that our only intelligent choice is to *believe* what is in the line of our needs.[18]

Have faith that you can successfully make it, and your feet are nerved to its accomplishment. But mistrust yourself, and think of all the sweet *[maybes]*, and you will hesitate so long that, at last, all unstrung and trembling, and launching yourself in a moment of despair, you roll in the abyss.[19]

## Choosing the Heroic Path

Each day I receive touching, inspiring letters from people who exhibit the courage and positive faith needed to succeed in holistic fashion. Their adherence in their business lives to whatever is worthy or sacred seems the essence of the spirituality that so often calls for sacrifice. To paraphrase one woman, who—when summoned by her vocation—reviewed the costs of creating her work:

At forty, I sold or gave away everything that wouldn't fit in my Toyota. I rented a small apartment in an older duplex that was drafty in winter and infested with cockroaches. Many mornings I drove to my graduate school courses with tears streaming down my face. It was one of the most challenging times of my adulthood. But I survived.

I completed a lengthy academic program in record time and even got straight A's, for the first time ever. This is my second week at my new job—my right livelihood. I now use all of myself, from my sales, executive, and marketing knowledge to my new counseling skills. My life is totally worth living.

I've written elsewhere that early in my teens, when my father died, I was left virtually alone.[20] Completely self-supporting through four tough years of undergraduate school, I barely got by academically or financially. It was then my deepest wish to earn a college degree, although at the time I couldn't have said why. I spent more hours each day at various part-time jobs than studying. Actually, I hated many of my classes, a fact which made my effort

177

to graduate all the more surprising. Recently, someone asked me to name my most fulfilling achievements. One that immediately came to mind was completing my bachelor's degree. Reviewing the comments of people quoted in this book, I know I'm not alone in feeling that lasting satisfaction is often a by-product of hardship. The entrepreneurial—and spiritual—relevance of all this seems obvious.

To create work you love, to build the life you want, your intellect must integrate *all* of its forces—rational and "irrational." This is how you gain power to achieve. Garnering wealth, inner and outer, depends on a logical *and* an artistic, transcendent mind, on faith *and* on worldly or technical competence. Spain's renowned Jesuit scholar, Baltasar Gracián—a keen observer of "good luck"— wrote that those who master their fortunes take a giant step forward as persons and manage their affairs as great artists.[21]

As you actively wrestle with today's problems, tomorrow's achievements fall into place. Your mind's honest encounter with reality (not how you wish things were) leads you toward the goals you cherish. What you *think* you're meant to do in life may well turn out (on the far side of experience) to be different from what you now expect. The well-worn adage that life is what happens while we're busy doing something else reinforces this. Participate with full engagement in whatever happens *now.*

I urge you precisely as I urge myself: Reach for your deepest joys. Heed what you genuinely need and value, here and now. Strengthen your good judgment, your discernment, so that you—and those you love—profit from the risks you take. Practice steadily to build technical, conceptual or social skills. Bit by intelligible bit, make choices that honor your healthiest instincts, your noble desires. This is how we build a life.

Attend to what Ben Shahn called the haunting fragments of your soul. How might you inject some lovely inner poetry of self into your daily work? How might you be discreetly kind to others through what you say and do? How might you persevere or extend your competence? Project your cherished ideas of love, truth, affluence, or service into *today's* acts and tomorrow will improve. This is creative spiritual work, and we were born to do it.

## A Final Word

Louis Lahr, former chairman of 3M tells a story which I paraphrase: An elementary teacher said to her tiny charges, "Boys and girls, today we're going to draw a picture of the imagination. Take out your crayons and let your mind run free." All the students—except one—began drawing. The girl sat thinking, apparently stymied. Finally, she announced, "I know what I'll draw. I'll draw a picture of God. He was pretty imaginative. After all, He created the whole world and everything in it." The horrified teacher said, "Oh, no, dear, you can't do that. No one knows what God looks like." The child thought another minute, then exclaimed, "You'll know what God looks like when I finish my assignment!"[22]

Our vocation *is* our life's assignment. To quote that little girl above, when we finish that job expertly—imaginatively, capably, and with love—our animating essence will shine through. That *light* is love, God within.

# Questions and Answers

Q:    *Can you say a bit more about what you call "spiritual intelligence" and say* how *it helps us find answers?*

A:    Spirituality means *spirit* or *Being:* Our unseen, animating essence. This includes wholesome desires, intuition, our ability to reconcile paradox, "whole-sight," visioning skills. All these and more help us meet daily obligations and solve problems. Schooling, career counselors, books, experts, the mixed signals that we get from a worldly, fluctuating society can only give us a torturous jumble of misleading, conflicting advice unless we cultivate and use our spiritual resources—our inner wisdom.

Each day requires a bit of transcendental dreaming, as John Muir put it. The workplace of assembly lines and pat answers is evaporating. Success now depends on thinking with a "whole brain," a full awareness. As suggested this is developed gradually—verbally and nonverbally—often through classic meditative disciplines, nature experiences or "peak" moments. People who grasp that right actions are not merely the linear, technically obvious ones, those who *use* all their mind's faculties have a creative edge.

Author Anthony J. Wilhem's touches on this issue in theological terms saying that our labors, (i.e., work, our struggle to find answers, etc.) become burdensome *because* we're divorced from our inner kingdom—separated from God. Having lost *ourselves,* we lose our way.

Q: *Your learning philosophy, if I can call it that, seems to include a heavy emphasis on observational exercises. Why is this? What's the developmental significance of this?*

A: *Our identifications matter:* What we store in our heads as images, ideas, and self-notions translate into life's externals. Let me give two specific examples.

Since childhood I've intentionally studied inspiring, disciplining stories about creatively gifted, self-actualizing people. I wanted creative freedom in my life and found examples (people I never met, by the way) of individuals who'd achieved it. This gave my mind patterns to emulate. Somehow, these became a template for my own professional expressions. As an educator, I've also observed students automatically doing much the same thing. Think of it: *You* learned to ride a bike by watching others ride bikes, not by dwelling how it would be to fall off. You learned to talk by listening to and mimicking your parents. That's not all there is to learning, but it's a natural start.

Percy Wells Cerutty, the noted Australian runner and trainer of Olympic champions like Herb Elliott (the first four-minute miler) had one, revolutionary goal: to help adult runners regain the fluid movements of childhood. Cerutty's methods were controversial. He required his athletes to have total commitment, to relearn (and unlearn) years of artificial, unproductive habits of movement. Many fine candidates quit along the way (much like many would-be entrepreneurs), causing him to say:

Man is deathly afraid to leave the artificial securities he has created for himself . . . This is why he is so slow to advance. New ideas aren't welcome. People are afraid of them. They're afraid to think for themselves and be original.[1]

Cerutty believed that by studying the movements of animals of every species, the brain would record the neural patterns of running freely. At seventy, Cerutty (who could still break a six-minute mile) said, "I've learned more from watching race horses than from any runner I've seen in any Olympic Games."[2]

Why do you think we look and talk and move like our parents (or whoever raised us)? Why do you think children who grow up in beautiful, liberating environments become healthier or more hopeful than those reared in crime-ridden, neglected conditions? Our eyes are photographers; our ears recorders. What we observe as possible—*for us*—becomes what we reach for.

Q: *Can you provide a concrete case-example of how someone used Positive Structuring to determine their* vocation:

A: A marketing executive with an excellent track record had little formal education. He worked for an upscale consumer-services company surrounded by peers with MBAs and Ph.D.s. He believed to succeed he'd have to earn a management degree, then go to a similar but smaller firm to move up the corporate ladder. This usually high-energy fellow wondered why he procrastinated in the pursuit of these goals. The longer we spoke, the more clearly I heard him defining success in corporate terms, not his own. He used college degrees and formal job titles as benchmarks for his life's worth.

When I commented on that, he willingly reexamined the issue. I asked him to summarize his goals subjectively (using his words and favorite images, not his management's) and do more research. His goals included travel, freedom, or a job in a foreign country. That, in effect, was his *"WHAT"*—his solution. Remember, Positive Structuring encompasses *three phases*: Defining "WHAT" (i.e., our goal or solution); incubating the WHAT; and exploring facets of WHAT through *lowrisk* prototypes or representations that give realistic feedback about the thing.*

Next, the executive incubated (played around with) and examined elements of these goals truthfully. This took time. Some of his "research" included:

---

*See *Developing A 21st Century Mind.*

- Listing his life's major fulfillments ("Defining Moments"), then identifying the pattern of these to determine *why* these brought satisfaction;
- Gathering photographs, memorabilia or written material he'd collected to see which values and aspirations might be hiding in these;
- Integrating the patterns of these fulfillments with his ten-year goal thus revising his *WHAT*—his overarching objective—along self-affirming lines.

His third set of activities happened only after this meandering "play" (incubation), after he discovered that nature (specifically landscaping English and Japanese gardens) had fascinated him all his life. He devoted all his spare time to travel and gardening. He read gardening and landscaping journals. His grandfather had been a famous landscaper who extolled the joys of gardening. Finally, this man admitted, "What I want most is financial freedom to travel, perhaps live in Japan or England and to design environments like those that have touched me. I'm only thirty-five, so I may as well shoot for what I really want." Acknowledging his truths let him move beyond other people's thinking. Now he freely merged his own interests with the realities of the job market. I must add, this took time. At this writing, he's still employed by the same company, saving and investing money. He plans to earn a landscaping degree over the next five years. His vocation involves growth and aesthetics—his own and others. He's using his day-to-day career pragmatically, to unfold who he really is.

Q: *How is the corporate world helping employees develop these inner resources?*

A: The best run companies provide ample educational opportunities for their employees to improve in three skills areas: technical, managerial, and creative (or personal). Some have fabulous in-house campuses, complete with world-class libraries and training staff. Some send teams of workers to off-site, learning centers. Most management teams get away once or twice a year for creative brainstorming sessions or, say, a wilderness experience. Increasingly, major corporations permit (or insist) that their long-term employees take sabbaticals. They realize that unfettered self-renewal promotes robust, high, self-initiated productivity. For instance, a friend at Intel recently returned to her fulltime job after a three months' sabbatical, during which she attended various conferences, college courses *and* studied acting.

You, too, may crave time off to test yourself in something new or simply to consider the realistic consequences of revising your occupation. This longing or restlessness is, at its deepest point, a spiritual call—an unseen and possibly *illogical* summons. The healthiest people admit they're careful about how they use free time. They choose real—authentic—fulfillments and friendships rather than phoney ones. To change your work, you may first have to scale back or relinquish a few creature comforts: a steady paycheck, the approval of others, a known career, a group of supportive colleagues. What *cannot* be seen—your spiritual and vocational raison d'etre—eventually becomes as significant as what *can* be seen.

Q: *You seem to be suggesting that as we use our "best" self, we grow more capable. Am I reading you correctly?*

A: Yes. Courtesy and wisdom (as opposed to academic or technical knowledge), good humor, all manner of virtues flourish when used. Follow your virtue, not just your bliss. I mention this because people frequently trivialize the word bliss. They easily confuse Joseph Campbell's edict, to "follow your bliss," as a pat recipe for situational happiness, mistakenly thinking that if they run after work that looks like "fun," they'll never again feel a twinge of pain or regret or have to struggle. Nothing could be more false. Leaving a secure job, we normally feel vulnerable and anxious. Separating from friends on a former work team, we naturally experience real grief. Virtues like faith, patience, perseverance, and love for our authentic occupation keep us moving forward toward "bliss." A paradox of "following bliss" is that the life we long to build rarely arrives instantly—it may be *un*blissful at first. Embracing this fact *is* somehow exhilarating.

In line with my corporate, human resource practice, I've met hundreds of aspiring leaders who blossom only after testing themselves in the arena of managing people. They don't *feel* blissful when resolving conflicts or conducting long meetings. Their gifts of influence increase through *use*. In other words, they are strengthened as whole persons by expressing virtues like courage or compassion. Later, they may experience the deep joy (and this *is* bliss) that comes from developing their potential. However, virtue leads the way and sustains us through the pain of that initial surrender to our inner call.

Our display of humor, ingenuity, or fundamental decency pleases *us*—and perhaps others. That pleasure is empowering, and exponentially furthers personal development. The man who confronts one longstanding falsehood, in time confronts others more easily. The individual who solves one problem alone soon discovers she's thinking independently in many areas.

Q: *This notion of viewing work as an art appeals to me. How do you do that?*

A: I've written that one of my favorite ways of finding direction for my own life is to spend a goodly chunk of quiet time each morning reading scripture.[3] Silence—for instance, the silence of a wilderness, the absence of speech—is, for me, profound. Meditating on a line or two of sacred writing I find enormously productive. Once, when fretting about whether or not to lessen my corporate involvements (so that I could write more) I came across a passage in Genesis where God advises Abram how to greet his own unknowns:

*Go forth from your country,*
*And from your relatives*
*And from your father's house,*
*To the land which I will show you;*
*And I will make you a great nation,*
*And I will bless you,*
*And make your name great;*
*And so you shall be a blessing . . .*[4]

A calm sureness accompanied my reading of these words: Entering my "wilderness" in faith could, eventually, allow me to *be* a blessing to others (not just have blessings). This idea encouraged me to alter my private practice. The verse uncovered a new, largely spiritual goal. We each need to find—and then trust—our *own* way.

Q:  *Please say a little more about how intuition might provide vocational direction.*

A:  As we strengthen it, our intuition lets us project—or communicate, as Ben Shahn put it—something inwardly substantial (like our sense of beauty or compassion) into the material world. A hunch or prompting may then influence our choices. Esther, mentioned in Chapter Seven, felt an impulse to get more involved in her church—at sixty or seventy! Shanalei felt a need to move from one state to another. Woody's heart was in carpentry, not in his engineering job. What are such feelings if not inner desires or haunting memory fragments, or remembrances of childhood pleasures, that inspired each to uproot their lives and create something new? These vague, even disturbing, emotions are all shades of intuition.

Perhaps, incomprehensibly, we'll gravitate toward a long vacation or graduate school. We may feel compelled to reveal something personal to a total stranger (like my airplane companion who told me about her son's dilemma). Out of our choice—our conversation—could come some helpful insight that we mull over all day (or dream about at night). The next morning, while shaving or showering, we know what we must do.

The pioneering contemporary sculptress Louise Nevelson once described her work as a love affair and a projected, life-long passion:

> Shakespeare said life is a stage and we all play a part . . . I liked that, that we project. Now when you project a world, the world is yours. . . . So you begin to be aware of your own creation. . . .
>
> I don't think that anyone's life is finished as long as they live. It's unfinished business. And I'm always looking, hoping to find another dimension, and I feel that I'm going to do some more things that I haven't thought of. . . . That's what living is. Look, darling, can you tell me how you're going to breathe tomorrow or the next day? As long as you live you can have more insight. That's the only reason, in a way, for living.
>
> You see, it unfolds more and more and more, and should— so you might, in a moment, see a whole eternity and vice versa. . . .[5]

Q: The authentic, "productive" person sounds like someone I'd like to be. Please give me an everyday example of that person's traits.

A: I recently met a contractor—a virtual stranger—who impressed me so much that I gave him a large remodeling job (without getting other, competitive bids). He exuded an attractive sureness. I later asked myself, what else was it that made me retain him? He seemed secure, focused, and without artifice. He cast off an "is-ness" or an intelligence. That too made me think he was dependable.

Some ancient texts suggest that the spiritually mature emit the light that's in them so that others may notice it. Abraham Maslow described self-actualizing adults as somehow "closer to their own nature," childlike and transparent yet simultaneously stable, mature, and seemingly reliable. The fully functioning productive person is also at ease:

> What takes effort, straining and struggling is . . . done without any sense of striving, of working or laboring, but "comes of itself." Allied to this often is the feeling of grace and the look of grace that comes with smooth, easy, effortless, full functioning, when everything "clicks" or "is in the groove" or is "in overdrive."
>
> One sees then the appearance of calm sureness and rightness, as if they knew exactly what they were doing, and were doing it wholeheartedly, without doubts, equivocations, hesitations, or partial withdrawal. . . . The great athletes, artists, creators, leaders, and executives exhibit this quality when they are functioning at their best.[6]

I observe a healthy, dynamic intensity in truly productive people: They're focused. They're fully present. They listen and watch what's happening—with all their forces, their entire being. When called upon to respond, to make a decision, to perform (even under pressure), they're relaxed, but as Harvey Penick puts it, " . . . ready."[7]

Q: *How might a corporate leader take a team of people from an "I can't" to an "I can" belief—turn negative thinking into positive faith?*

A: It's a little like what we used to call "Chinese water torture": continual, repetitive drops along a consciously intended line. *Repetition* of an idea will change your mind. A tiny start-up firm hired a core of gifted marketing and sales people. I was retained to help structure positive self-beliefs ("I can" attitudes) and spirited team cohesion. We held monthly strategic and motivational sessions to maintain disciplined focus and upbeat cooperation. Everyone studied and understood the Positive Structuring method.

Periodically, the CEO distributed inspirational essays on the power and techniques of success-thinking. These essays served as *drops of water*. The whole company regularly celebrated its benchmark achievements. More *drops of water*. Despite this, staff members still experienced anxiety (when, for example, their sales calls were rejected or when prospective clients canceled meetings). There were ample opportunities to worry. *What if* this venture failed? *What if* the sales efforts failed? *What if* the team—or the whole company—failed? The founder gracefully forged ahead. Daily, he illustrated how to *function despite uncertainty*. His way of being was like *drops of water*. He focused on one task at a time. He never spoke of possible financial loss. The others marveled at this but couldn't quite duplicate his faith, his single-mindedness. Suddenly, one talented young man experienced an epiphany of sorts:

> I see what I need! To build a belief that my goals are possible for me. I tend to doubt the availability of my good—I question the durability of things that are "too good to be true," feel my achievement bubble will burst, or that I won't have what it takes to sustain whatever I most wanted to accomplish. Mine is a mental battle—not an external one!

Almost everyone who creates effectively in some uncharted region eventually discovers their beliefs *shape* their outcomes. The true heros and heroines of the world show us that, despite the hazards of a worthwhile risk, positive faith *beforehand* makes their results probable.

Q:    *I'm impatient to see results. I get disheartened when I read that it might take me a long time to create a business. How do I get over this?*

A:    Someone once said that the secret of success is to put your whole self into *all* your small acts. The 6th-century sage Lao-tzu acknowledged this, saying "great acts are made up of small deeds."

Patience occurs in awareness first. When you realize that your small, inconsequential steps are *ends* in themselves—taking you where you want to go, epitomizing your goal, letting you taste your good immediately—you'll experience the satisfaction of results, right now. Just as a sage achieves greatness by taking care of business here and now, so can you build your ventures with little, productive choices that *embody* your larger goal. See daily tasks and choices as both ends *and* means: These are like a "seed within itself," as the Bible puts it. These profit you now (because you savor a bit of what you love) and later when your good has multiplied. A parent who loves his child speaks to it tenderly every day and doesn't wait until the child has graduated from college to be loving. Then it's too late. The carpenter who loves beautiful wood uses it now, whenever possible; she doesn't wait until she's constructed a mass of shoddy tables. *Be* and *do* what you love today, this instant, here and now. Your end is born in the beginning in every small act.

Q: *Please give me another case example of how someone used a crisis or loss to gain insight.*

A: Our sustained involvement in some dilemma or theme pierces the veil of appearances. At first glance, our problems may seem insurmountable. Deep, truthful focus is the precursor to those clarifying shifts-of-mind that reveal what's possible. When a friend was driving alone to his mother's funeral, somberly mulling over the turmoil he'd experienced that year—caring for a seriously ill spouse and a dying parent, earning only dismal revenues due to a sick economy—he had an insight:

> I "saw" myself traveling down a dark, unfriendly road as a result of my screwed-up choices. Then, my mind's eye noticed a path with many offshoot trails leading here and there. Immediately in my head I heard, "Carve out a new path; take action for improved directions. Let go of the rest." And that's what I've done.

Q: *Could you add a word about managing stress and its relationship to the creative process? What do you do to manage your energy?*

A: When under pressure—or coming up with new ideas—I watch old movies, take long drives, or prune roses in my garden. I've already said that I love silence, that I read scripture. I rarely work at night. Twice I've taken a year's sabbatical—essentially to "do nothing." Each time this time off has transformed my approach to work. Most healthy executives walk, jog, or swim daily. Some regularly attend health spas. I rarely meet senior managers who don't depend on either easy-going golf games or strenuous tennis sessions or short catnaps to manage stress and solve problems. Rest and renewal are essential daily companions which boost creative drive. Only fools ignore this fact.

The former Secretary of Health, Education and Welfare and prolific author, John Gardner, believes that self-renewal is a leader's most potent and critical task. As this relates to work, people with the wherewithal to create their livelihoods are, at minimum, leaders within the sphere of their own lives. Creating work could easily turn us into people who don't know when enough's enough. To be successful we must adopt Gardner's self-renewal dictum as our own. Each of us can devise our own ways to play, to regenerate ourselves and enjoy life.

Q: *I want to start a home-based business. Please tell me more about those strong mental muscles you talk about. What else can I read to learn about the technical side of all this?*

A: In addition to the books already mentioned (e.g., by Hawkins, by Fritz, by Touchie), authors Philips and Rasberry provide financial and technical strategies they call "tradeskills" in *Honest Business:* "persistence, ability to face facts, knowing how to minimize risks, and being a hands-on learner."[8] Also, cowriting with Claude Whitmeyer, they interview eight, successful one-person business owners to flesh out yet more specific skills and traits.[9] Related to the planning and positioning issues raised in

Chapter Six, you'll find concrete recommendations for a marketing plan in Jay Conrad Levinson's *Guerrilla Marketing*. In discussing positioning we learn:

> . . . No guerrilla would think of doing one speck of marketing without a proper marketing plan that includes a positioning statement. . . .
>
> . . . If you want, you can make your finished plan up to ten pages long. But at first, try stating it in one paragraph. Suppose you call your business Prosper Press and you intend to sell books about freelancing. Let your paragraph start with the words:
>
> "The purpose of Prosper Press marketing is to sell the maximum number of books at the lowest possible selling cost per book. The target market will be people who can or do engage in free-lance earning activities."[10]

Also, let the bibliography in any valuable book lead you further. Notice what quoted passages you enjoy; follow their trail to those author's works. Think *support systems* too: what adult education classes, YMCA or YWCA or Junior Achievement or Chamber of Commerce programs might you find (or start) to surround yourself with like-minded enthusiasts? I recommend weekly or at minimum monthly study-circles, led by trained facilitators, to "chew on" the ideas in a good nonfiction book, chapter by chapter, before trying to implement these. These groups keep motivation high.

Q: *It's pleasing to think I can grow whole using daily acts as my vehicle. How do we do that?*

A: You probably already know *exactly* what to do: Make that tough phone call; order a college catalogue; sign up for your high-school equivalency course; enroll in a literacy, sales training, or health-care course. Communicate some caring or compassionate message to others through what you *do*—not just what you say. Unfold your finest humanity in small, steady choices so that practical, community-serving (and even profitable) accomplishments become yours. *Notice* others of all ages and abilities who do this.

If you look, you'll find books, seminars, support groups, adult education programs and people everywhere to help you. Our era offers unlimited opportunity and support for such efforts. Perhaps you'll slip or stall, take longer to figure out (or reach) your goals than you first planned. What of it? At such times, Ray Bradbury's counsel helps me regain buoyancy: "if you're going to step on a live mine, make it your own. Be blown up, as it were, by your *own* delights and despairs."[11]

Pay attention intelligently. You'll notice your worst blunders rich with subtle truths—signposts pointing you upward, to vitality or healthy connections with others. (What else is spirituality if not élan vital—your hot, healthiest animating essence?) After setbacks, rest a bit. Pray a bit. Forgive a lot. Sort things out a bit with a trusted counselor. Then, get up and begin again.

*Let your truths lead you.* If you're brave enough, if you're entrepreneurial enough, you *can* invent your way to purposeful, appropriate material gain *and* self-realization—two goals worthy of your time and effort. Your self-disciplined ability to *"Hear a word behind thee, saying 'This is the way'"* is unequivocally an element of what I'm describing. Some call this prayer. Others might call this attending to the heart or to values. Whatever words you choose, invest your talents faithfully, prudently, *lovingly* in what you respect and want. In time you'll reap inexhaustible rewards.

# END NOTES

## Introduction

1. Gallup Organization, *Newsweek,* January 28, 1993, (Roper Center; University of Connecticut).

2. Marsha Sinetar, *Developing a 21st Century Mind* (New York: Villard Books, 1991).

## From Chapter One

1. Marsha Sinetar, *Developing a 21st Century Mind* (New York: Villard, 1991).

2. *New Webster's Dictionary* (New York: Delair Publishing, 1981).

3. *U. S. News & World Report* (December 27, 1993): 40.

4. *60 Minutes,* "It's the Economy, Stupid," CBS interview transcript (February 14, 1993).

5. David Viscott, M.D., *The Language of Feelings* (New York: Pocket Books, 1976).

6. Warren Midgett, "Jogging in a Jug," *Forbes* (July 19, 1993): 71.

7. Joel Kotkin, "The American Way," *Inc.* (September 1991).

8. Bill Mandel, "Barbeque: The Link to Success," *San Francisco Examiner,* (July 25, 1993): B1, B2.

9. Ibid.

10. Howard Rheingold, *They Have a Word for It* (New York: J. P. Tarcher, Inc., 1988): 90.

11. Ibid.

12. J. H. Brennan, *Getting What You Want* (New York: Stein and Day, 1974): 26.


*From Chapter Two*

1. From Dr. Herman J. Aaftink's lecture, *The Paraclete*, QF #488, available from Calgary Life Enrichment Centre, Calgary, Alberta, Canada.

2. Abraham Maslow, *Toward a Psychology of Being* (New York: D. Van Nostrand Co., 1962).

3. John Briggs, *Fire in the Crucible* (Los Angeles: J. P. Tarcher, Inc., 1990), 72.

4. Fernando Mateo, *Pinnacle*, CNN Transcript #176, (August 29, 1993). Can be obtained from Journal Graphics, Inc., 1535 Grant Street, Denver, CO 80203.

5. Briggs, *Fire in the Crucible*, 203.

6. Abraham Maslow, *The Farther Reaches of Human Nature* (New York: Viking, 1971).

7. Clark Moustakas, *The Authentic Teacher* (Cambridge, Massachusetts: Howard Doyle Co., 1966), 5.

8. Alice Miller, *The Drama of the Gifted Child* (New York: Basic Books, Inc., 1981).

9. Paul Hughes, "Big Ideas," *Business Start-Ups* (August 1993): 40.

10. Warren Midgett, "Jogging in a Jug," *Forbes* (July 19, 1993).

11. Fernando Mateo, *Pinnacle*, CNN.

12. Harvey Penick and Bud Shrake, *Harvey Penick's Little Red Book* (New York: Simon & Schuster, 1992), 161.

13. *Cure Now (Praxis):* Post Office Box 29386, Los Angeles, California 90029. (This magazine may now be out of print.)

14. Anthony De Mello, *One-Minute Wisdom* (New York: Image/ Doubleday, 1985).


*From Chapter Three*

1. *60 Minutes,* "It's the Economy, Stupid," CBS (February 14, 1993).

2. Ibid.

3. Marsha Sinetar, "Right Livelihood in a Recession?," *Common Boundary* (1991).

4. D. B. Phillips, E. B. Howes, and L. Nixon, *The Choice Is Always Ours* (Wheaton, Illinois: ReQuest Books, 1977), 188.

5. Anthony De Mello, *One-Minute Wisdom* (New York: Image/ Doubleday, 1985), 94.

6. Marsha Sinetar, *Do What You Love, The Money Will Follow* (New York: Dell, 1989), pp. 82–119.

7. Brian O'Reilly, "Depressed? Here's Help," *Reader's Digest* (condensed from *Fortune*) (April 1994): 152.

8. R. L. Wing, *The I Ching Workbook* (New York: Doubleday & Co., 1979), 39.

9. "Tale from Dropout Hell," *Smart Money* (April 15, 1992): 108–114.

10. Ibid.

11. Fritz Perls, *Ego, Hunger & Aggression* (New York: Vintage Books, 1969), 55.

12. Marsha Sinetar, *Reel Power* (New York: Liguori/Triumph Books, Liguori, Missouri, 1993).

13. Ibid.

14. Marsha Sinetar, *Do What You Love, The Money Will Follow* (Mahwah, New Jersey: Paulist Press, 1989).

15. St. Matthew 25:19, *King James Bible*.


*From Chapter Four*

1. E. Paul Torrance, *Guiding Creative Talent* (New Jersey: Prentice-Hall, 1962), 120.

2. Rheingold, *They Have a Word for It.*

3. Marsha Sinetar, *Developing a 21st Century Mind* (New York: Villard Books, 1991), 60. For a lengthy discussion of this, see Chapter 3, *Developing a 21st Century Mind,* for numerous case examples, including that of co-creator of *Logo* (a children's computer game), Seymour Papert, who says, "Before I was two years old, I developed an intense involvement with automobiles [and gears] . . . and [later] became adept at turning wheels in my head and at making chains of cause and effect." See also Seymour Papert's book, below.

4. Seymour Papert, *Mindstorms* (New York: Basic Books, 1980), p. vi.

5. E. Torrance, *Guiding Creative Talent.*

6. Alan Liere, "Originals & One-of-a-Kinds," *Washington,* vol. 4, no. 5 (January/February 1988): 72.

7. Ibid.

8. Roger Ailes, "Break the Rules and Win," *Success* (January/February 1994): 37.

9. Edward deBono, *Tactics* (Toronto-Boston: Little, Brown and Co., 1984), 93.

10. Sinetar, *Developing a 21st Century Mind.*

11. Marsha Sinetar, *Living Happily Ever After* (New York: Villard Books, 1990).

12. Note that Quimby's ideas have been well preserved and documented and that his legacy lives on, among other places at Calgary Life Enrichment Center (Calgary, Alberta) whose founder, Dr. Herman J. Aaftink, is a foremost Quimby authority.

13. Dennis Kimbro and Napoleon Hill, "Profiting Through Self-Reliance," *Black Enterprise,* v. 23 (November 1992): 105–106.

14. Ibid.

15. Stephanie Irving, *Washington,* vol. 4, no. 5 (January/February 1988): 74.

16. I *think* I heard Ben Kingsley say this in an interview (on PBS, A&E, or CNN) but can't swear to it.

17. Sinetar, *Developing a 21st Century Mind.*

18. Frances E. Willard, *How I Learned to Ride the Bicycle* (Sunnyvale, California: Fair Oaks Publishing, 1991), 37.

19. Sinetar, *Living Happily Ever After.*

20. Sinetar, *Developing a 21st Century Mind.*

21. Vera John-Steiner, *Notebooks of the Mind* (New York: Harper Perennial Library, 1987).

22. Alan Lakein, *How to Get Control of Your Time and Your Life* (New York: Signet/New American Library, 1973), 37–39.

23. Ibid.

*From Chapter Five*

1. Stanley Coopersmith, *The Antecedents of Self-Esteem* (San Francisco: W. H. Freeman & Co., 1967).

2. Edward deBono, *Tactics* (Toronto-Boston: Little, Brown and Company, 1984).

3. Florida Scott-Maxwell, *The Measure of My Days* (New York: Penguin Books, 1968), 21.

4. David Frost/Isaac Stern Interview; PBS Transcript #21 (November 27, 1992) DPTV Productions and GWETA. Can be obtained from Journal Graphics, 1535 Grant Street, Denver, CO 80203.

5. Ibid.

6. Peter Matthiessen, *Nine-Headed Dragon River* (Boston: Shambala, 1986), 60.

7. Dr. Paul Yonggi Cho, *How to Make Success In Your King's Business,* Audio AC2-2. Can be obtained from FGBMFT (Tape Services Division), PO Box 5050, Costa Mesa, CA 92628.

8. Thomas Merton, *The Way of Chuang Tzu* (Boston: Shambala, 1992), 76.

9. Thomas Cleary, *Zen Essence* (Boston: Shambala, 1989), 61.

10. Marsha Sinetar, *Developing a 21st Century Mind* (New York: Villard, 1991).

11. Maria Montessori, *Dr. Montessori's Own Handbook* (New York: Schocken Books, 1965), 71.

12. Harvey Penick and Bud Shrake, *Harvey Penick's Little Red Book* (New York: Simon & Schuster, 1992).

13. David Shapiro, *Autonomy and Rigid Character* (New York: Basic Books, 1981), 81.

14. Paul Hawkens, *Growing A Business* (New York: Simon Schuster, 1987), 91.

*From Chapter Six*

1. I. A. Horowitz and Fred Reinfeld, *How to Improve Your Chess* (New York: Collier Books, 1972).

2. Abraham Maslow, *Toward A Psychology of Being* (New York: D. Van Nostrand Co., 1962).

3. Alvin Toffler, *The Adaptive Corporation* (New York: McGraw-Hill Books, 1985), 23.

4. Horowitz and Reinfeld, *How to Improve Your Chess,* 91.

5. Edward R. Tufte, *Envisioning Information* (Graphics Press: Cheshire, Conn., 1990).

6. *The Dick Cavett Show,* CNBC interview (May 28, 1993).

7. Casey Bush, *Grandmaster from Oregon: The Life & Games of Arthur Dake* (Portland, Oregon: Portland Chess Press, 1991).

8. *Lombardi: Winning Is the Only Thing,* Jerry Kramer, ed. (New York: The World Publishing Co., 1971), 91.

9. Eugen Herrigel, *Zen in the Art of Archery* (New York: Vintage Books, 1971), 74.

10. Edward deBono, *Tactics* (Toronto-Boston: Little, Brown, and Co., 1984).

11. Fernando Mateo, *Pinnacle,* CNN Transcript #176 (August 29, 1993). Can be obtained from Journal Graphis, Inc., 1535 Grant Street, Denver, CO 80203.

12. Roger Fritz, *Nobody Gets Rich Working for Somebody Else,* (Menlo Park, California: Crisp Publications, 1993).

13. Rodger Touchie, *Preparing a Successful Business Plan* (Bellingham, Washington: Self-Counsel Press, 1993).

14. Warren Bennis and Burt Nanus, *Leaders* (New York: Harper Perennial, 1985), 103.

15. Maria Montessori, *Dr. Montessori's Own Handbook* (New York: Schocken Books, 1965), 58.

16. Ibid.

17. Marsha Sinetar, *Developing a 21st Century Mind* (New York: Villard Books, 1991), 73.

18. George Dudley and Shannon Goodson, *The Psychology of Call Reluctance* (Dallas: Behavioral Science Research Press, 1986), 7.

19. Dennis Kimbro and Napoleon Hill, "Profiting Through Self-Reliance," *Black Enterprise* (November 1992): 105–106.

20. Al Ries and Jack Trout, *Positioning: The Battle for Your Mind* (New York: Warner Books, 1981).

21. I first heard this story told on tape by Dr. Frederick Eikerenkoetter—Reverend Ike. (Science of Living Publications, Box 130, Brookline, MA 02146.) It may have originated in his *Health, Happiness and Prosperity—For You!* Edition #TW0010482, SOL Publications, 1982, Science of Living Institute, p. 175.

22. David Viscott, M.D., *The Language of Feelings* (New York: Pocket Books, 1976).

*From Chapter Seven*

1. Marsha Sinetar, *Ordinary People as Monks and Mystics* (Mahwah, New Jersey: Paulist Press, 1986).

2. A. Reza Aresteh, *Anxious Search: The Way to Universal Self* (Institute of Perspective Analysis).

3. Thomas Cleary, *Zen Essence* (Boston: Shambala, 1989).

4. Peter Browning, *John Muir, In His Own Words* (Lafayette, California: Great West Books, 1988), 25.

5. Acts 9:3–4, *King James Bible*.

6. Abraham Maslow, *The Farther Reaches of Human Nature,* (New York: Viking Press, 1971).

7. John D. Morse, ed., *Ben Shahn,* (New York: Praeger Publishers, 1972), p. 200.

8. Ibid., p. 197.

9. W. J. Weatherby, *Chariots of Fire* (New York: Dell/Quicksilver, 1981), 16, 86–87.

10. Ibid.

11. John Briggs, *Fire In the Crucible* (Los Angeles: J. P. Tarcher, 1990), 13.

12. Ibid., p. 201.

13. Ibid., p. 239.

14. *Familiar Quotations by John Bartlett,* 14th edition (Little Brown & Co., Boston, 1968), p. 928. Robert Frost, "Two Tramps in Mud Time" (1936 stanza three).

15. Marsha Sinetar, *A Way Without Words* (Mahwah, New Jersey: Paulist Press, 1992).

16. Ibid., p. 16.

17. *The Portable Tolstoy,* ed. John Bayley (New York: Viking Penguin, 1978), 683.

18. William James, *The Will to Believe* (New York: Dover Publications, 1956), 59.

19. Ibid.

20. Marsha Sinetar, *Living Happily Ever After,* (New York: Villard Books, 1990), p.

21. Baltasar Gracián, *The Art of Worldly Wisdom,* Christopher Maurer, trans. (New York: Doubleday-Currency Books, 1992).

22. Lewis Lahr, *The Care and Feeding of Innovators,* Summer 1987, taped lecture. Can be obtained from The Chautauqua Institution, Chautauqua, NY 14722.

*From Afterword*

1. Larry Myers, *Training with Cerutty* (Mountain View, California: World Publications, 1977), 40.

2. Ibid.

3. Marsha Sinetar, *A Way Without Words* (Mahway, New Jersey: Paulist Press, 1991).

4. Genesis 1:1–3, *King James Bible.*

5. Louise Nevelson, *A Conversation with Barbaralee Diamonstein,* (New York: The Pace Gallery, 1980).

6. Abraham Maslow, *Toward a Psychology of Being* (New York: D. Van Nostrand Co., 1962), 100.

7. Harvey Penick and Bud Shrake, *Harvey Penick's Little Red Book* (New York: Simon & Schuster, 1992).

8. Michael Philips and Salli Rasberry, *Honest Business (A Superior Strategy for Starting and Managing Your Own Business)* (New York: Random House, 1981).

9. Claude Whitmeyer, Salli Rasberry, and Michael Philips, *Running a One Person Business* (Berkeley, California: Ten Speed Press, 1989.)

10. Jay Conrad Levinson, *Guerrilla Marketing* (Boston: Houghton Mifflin Company, 1984).

11. Ray Bradbury, *Zen in the Art of Writing* (New York: Bantam Books, 1990), 15.

# BIBLIOGRAPHY

Dr. Herman J. Aaftink, *The Paraclete,* Lecture QF #488, Available from Calgary Life Enrichment Centre, Calgary, Alberta, Canada T2J 6A8.

Roger Ailes, "Break the Rules and Win," *Success,* January/February 1994, p. 37.

A. Reza Aresteh, *Anxious Search,* Institute of Perspective Analysis (no date, no publication location available).

John Bayley, ed. *The Portable Tolstoy,* New York: Viking Penguin, Inc. 1978, pp. 122 and 683.

Warren Bennis and Burt Nanus, *Leaders,* New York: Harper & Row Perennial, 1985, p. 103.

Richard N. Bolles, *How to Find Your Mission in Life,* Berkeley, California: Ten Speed Press, 1991.

J. H. Brennan, *Getting What You Want,* New York: Stein and Day, 1974, p. 26.

Ray Bradbury, *Zen in the Art of Writing,* New York: Bantam Books, 1990, p. 15.

John Briggs, *Fire in the Crucible,* Los Angeles: Jeremy P. Tarcher, Inc., 1990, pp. 13, 72, 203.

Anita Brown, "Centering In," *Inside Minority Business,* January 25, 1993, p. 22.

Peter Browning, *John Muir, In His Own Words,* Lafayette, California: Great West Books, 1988, p. 25.

Martin Buber, *The Way of Response* (ed. N. N. Glatzer), New York: Schocken Books, 1966.

Casey Bush, *Grandmaster from Oregon: The Life & Games of Arthur Dake,* Portland, Oregon: Portland Chess Press, 1991.

Thomas Cleary, *Zen Essence,* Boston: Shambala, 1989, p. 61.

Stanley Coopersmith, *The Antecedents of Self-Esteem,* San Francisco: W. H. Freeman & Co., 1967.

*Cure Now (Praxis):* Post Office Box 29386, Los Angeles, California 90029.

Edward deBono, *Tactics: The Art and Science of Success,* Boston: Little Brown; Toronto-Boston: Little, Brown and Company, 1984, p. 93.

Anthony De Mello, *One Minute Wisdom,* New York: Image/Double-day, 1985, p. 94.

*The Dick Cavett Show,* CNBC interview, May 28, 1993, 6:00 P.M.

Genesis 1:1–3.

George Dudley; Shannon Goodson, *The Psychology of Call Reluctance,* Dallas: Behavioral Science Research Press, 1986, p. 7.

Henry Fairlie, *The New Republic,* vol. 200, No. 14, issue 3862, January 23, 1989, Washington, D.C. 20036, p. 14.

William Frank and Charles Lapp, *How to Outsell the Born Salesman,* New York: Collier Books, 1967.

Roger Fritz, *Nobody Gets Rich Working for Somebody Else,* Crisp Publications, 1993.

David Frost/Isaac Stern Interview; PBS; air date November 27, 1992, DPTV Productions and GWETA; Transcript #21, *Journal Graphics* (pp. 4 and 5).

Robert Frost, "Two Tramps in Mud Time," *Familiar Quotations by John Bartlett,* 14th ed., Boston: Little Brown & Co., 1968, p. 928.

Gallup Organization, *Newsweek,* January 28, 1993, (Roper Center; University of Connecticut).

John Gardner, *Excellence,* New York: Harper & Row, 1962, p. 132.

William Glasser, M.D., *Positive Addiction,* New York: Harper & Row, 1976.

Baltasar Gracián, *The Art of Worldly Wisdom,* translated by Christopher Maurer, New York: Doubleday-Currency Books, 1992.

Louis Harris and Associates, *The Kaiser Family Foundation, The Commonwealth Fund,* January 31, 1992, (Roper Center; University of Connecticut).

Phillip R. Harris, *Management in Transition,* New York: Jossey-Bass, 1985.

Paul Hawkens, *Growing a Business,* New York: Simon Schuster, 1987, p. 91.

Eugen Herrigel, *Zen in the Art of Archery,* New York: Vintage Books, Random House, 1971, p. 74.

I. A. Horowitz and Fred Reinfeld, *How to Improve Your Chess,* New York: Collier Books, 1972, p. 91.

Paul Hughes, "Big Ideas," *Business Start-Ups,* Irvine, California: Entrepreneur Media, Inc., August 1993, p. 40.

*International Thesaurus of Quotations* (compiled, Rhoda Thomas Tripp), New York: Thomas Crowell Co., 1970.

Stephanie Irving, *Washington,* Vol. 4; No. 5; Jan–Feb 1988, p. 74.

*King James Bible,* Acts 9:3–4.

William James, *The Will To Believe,* New York: Dover Publications, Inc. 1956, p. 59.

Vera John-Steiner, *Notebooks of the Mind,* New York: (Harper & Row) Perennial Library, 1987.

Sidney M. Jourard, *The Transparent Self,* New York: Van Nostrand Reinhold & Co., 1971, p. 5.

Ralph H. Kilmann, *Beyond the Quick Fix,* New York: Jossey-Bass, 1985.

Dennis Kimbro and Napolean Hill, "Profiting Through Self-Reliance," *Black Enterprise,* V. 23, November 1992, pp. 105 and 106.

Joel Kotkin, "The American Way," *Inc.,* September 1991.

Lewis Lahr, *The Care and Feeding of Innovators,* taped lecture available from The Chautauqua Institution, Chautauqua, New York 14722, summer 1987.

Alan Lakein, *How to Get Control of Your Time and Your Life,* New York: Signet/New American Library, 1973, pp. 37, 38, 39.

Jay Conrad Levinson, *Guerrilla Marketing,* Boston: Houghton Mifflin Co., 1984, p. 22.

Alan Liere, "Originals & One-of-a-Kinds," *Washington,* Vol. 4: No. 5; Jan–Feb 1988, p. 72.

Robert Lindner, *Prescription for Rebellion,* New York: Grove Press, 1962.

*Lombardi: Winning Is the Only Thing,* ed. Jerry Kramer, New York: The World Publishing Co., 1971, p. 91.

Bill Mandel, "Barbeque: The Link to Success," *San Francisco Examiner,* Metro Section; Sunday, July 25, 1993, pp. B1, B2.

Abraham Maslow, *The Farther Reaches of Human Nature,* New York: Esalen Book, Viking Press, 1971, p. 183.

Abraham Maslow, *Toward a Psychology of Being,* New York: D. Van Nostrand Co., 1962, p. 100.

Fernando Mateo, *Pinnacle,* CNN, August 29, 1993 (Transcript #176) available from *Journal Graphics,* 1535 Grant Street, Denver, Colorado 80203.

Peter Matthiessen, *Nine-Headed Dragon River,* Boston: Shambala 1986, p. 60.

Rollo May, *Courage to Create,* Bantam Books, 1976, p. 149.

Thomas Merton, *The Way of Chuang Tzu,* Boston, Shambala Pocket Classic, 1992, p. 76.

Warren Midgett, "Jogging in a Jug," *Forbes,* July 19, 1993, p. 71.

Alice Miller, *The Drama of the Gifted Child,* trans. Ruth Ward, New York: Basic Books, Inc., 1981.

Arthur F. Miller; Ralph T. Mattson, *The Truth About You,* Old Tappan, New Jersey: Fleming H. Revell, 1977, p. 23.

Clark Moustakas, *The Authentic Teacher,* Cambridge, Massachusetts: Howard Doyle Co., 1966, (*See* p. 5 for case illustration).

Maria Montessori, *Dr. Montessori's Own Handbook,* New York: Schocken Books, 1965 p. 71.

John D. Morse, ed., *Ben Shahn,* New York: Praeger Pub., Inc., 1972, p. 197.

Larry Myers, *Training with Cerutty,* Mountain View, California: World Publications, 1977, p. 40.

Louise Nevelson, *A Conversation with Barbaralee Diamonstein,* New York: The Pace Gallery, May–June 1980.

*New Webster's Dictionary,* New York: Delair Publishing, 1981.

Brian O'Reilly, "Depressed? Here's Help," (condensed from *Fortune*) *Reader's Digest,* April 1994, p. 152.

Ron Owens Show, KGO Talk-Radio, San Francisco, April 15, 1993.

Seymour Papert, *Mindstorms,* New York: Basic Books, 1980, p. vi.

Harvey Penick and Bud Shrake, *Harvey Penick's Little Red Book,* New York: Simon & Schuster, 1992, p. 161.

Fritz Perls, *Ego, Hunger & Aggression,* New York, New York: Vintage Books, 1969, p. 55.

Tom Peters, "Seek Mastery of Your Job—Be It Barn-Cleaning or Carmaking," *San Jose Mercury News,* Section D, Monday, May 17, 1993.

D. B. Philips, E. B. Howes, and L. Nixon, *The Choice Is Always Ours,* Wheaton, Illinois: ReQuest Books, 1977, p. 188

Michael Philips and Salli Rasberry, *Honest Business,* San Francisco: Clear Glass Publishing; New York: Random House, 1981, p. 14.

Gifford Pinchot III, *Intrapreneuring,* New York: Harper & Row, 1985, p. 228.

Princeton Survey Research Associates, *U. S. News & World Report,* January 12, 1993 (Roper Center, University of Connecticut).

Howard Rheingold, *They Have a Word for It,* New York and Los Angeles: Jeremy P. Tarcher, Inc., 1988, p. 90.

Al Ries and Jack Trout, *Positioning: The Battle for Your Mind,* New York: Warner Books, 1981.

St. Matthew 25:19, *King James Bible.*

Florida Scott-Maxwell, *The Measure of My Days,* New York: Penguin Books, 1968, p. 21.

*Ben Shahn,* ed. John D. Morse, New York: Praeger Publishers, 1972, p. 200.

David Shapiro, *Autonomy and Rigid Character,* New York: Basic Books, 1981.

Marsha Sinetar, *Developing a 21st Century Mind,* New York: Villard Books, 1991 pp. 60 and 73, [Ballantine Books, 1992], [Ballantine/Fawcett (Random House), 1992].

Marsha Sinetar, *Do What You Love, The Money Will Follow,* New York, New York: Dell, 1989.

Marsha Sinetar, *Living Happily Ever After* (Chapter 1), New York: Villard Books, 1990.

Marsha Sinetar, *Ordinary People as Monks and Mystics,* Mahwah, New Jersey: Paulist Press, 1986.

Marsha Sinetar, *Reel Power,* New York: Liguori/Triumph Books, Liguori, Missouri, 1993.

Marsha Sinetar, "Right Livelihood in a Recession?", *Common Boundary,* Cambridge, Massachusetts, July–August 1992.

Marsha Sinetar, *A Way Without Words,* Mahwah, New Jersey: Paulist Press, 1991, p. 16.

*60 Minutes,* "It's The Economy, Stupid," CBS (interview transcript): February 14, 1993.

*Swell! Living Well with Arthritis,* Colorado Springs, CO 80934: Charles Fowler publisher.

"Tale from Dropout Hell," in *Smart Money,* New York: Wall Street Journal/Hearst Corp./Dow Jones & Co., Inc., April 15, 1992, pp. 108–114 (p. 109 quote).

Lionel Tiger, *Optimism: The Biology of Hope,* New York: Simon & Schuster, 1979.

Alvin Toffler, *The Adaptive Corporation,* New York: McGraw-Hill Books, 1985, p. 23.

E. Paul Torrance, *Guiding Creative Talent,* New Jersey: Prentice-Hall, 1962, p. 120.

Rodger Touchie, *Preparing a Successful Business Plan,* Bellingham, Washington: Self-Counsel Press, 1993.

Edward R. Tufte, *Envisioning Information,* Box 430, Cheshire, Connecticut 06410: Graphics Press.

*U.S. News & World Report,* December 27, 1993–January 3, 1994, p. 40.

David Viscott, M.D., *The Language of Feelings,* New York: Pocket Books, 1976.

Dr. An Wang (with Eugene Linden), *Lessons,* Menlo Park, California: Addison-Wesley Publishing Company, Inc., 1986, p. 11.

W. J. Weatherby, *Chariots of Fire,* New York: Dell/Quicksilver, 1981, p. 16; pp. 86–87.

Frances E. Willard, *How I Learned to Ride the Bicycle,* ed. Carol O'Hare, Sunnyvale, California: Fair Oaks Publishing, 1991, p. 37.

Claude Whitmeyer, Salli Rasberry, and Michael Philips, *Running a One Person Business,* Berkeley, California. Ten Speed Press, 1989.

R. L. Wing, *The I Ching Workbook,* New York: Doubleday & Co., 1979, v. 39.

"Working," Martha Stewart, *Living,* April–May 1993, No. 13, New York: Time Publishing, p. 6.

*Work in Progress* transcript, CNN, June 2, 1993.

*World News* (Special Report), CNN, May 31, 1993, 7:15 P.M.

Dr. Paul Yonggi Cho, *How to Make Success In Your King's Business,* Audio AC2-2, FGBMFT (Tape Services Division) Post Office Box 5050, Costa Mesa, California 92628.